OF SOLIDS
AND SURDS

Notes for Noël Sturgeon, Marilyn Hacker,*
Josh Lukin, Mia Wolff, Bill Stribling,
and Bob White

SAMUEL R. DELANY

THE 2020 WINDHAM-CAMPBELL LECTURE

YALE UNIVERSITY PRESS
NEW HAVEN AND LONDON

---

*[CopyEd:] *I had the pleasure of editing two of Marilyn's translations for the Press: the poems of Hédi Kaddour and the poems of Jean-Paul de Dadelsen. I believe that a comment about its being a small world might be in order!*
[SRD:] By all means, if you will allow me to include some of our exchanges. I believe a lot of people who read books like this don't realize how small the combined world of writers and editors at various levels can be. Both Lukin and Stribling are here in memoriam.

The *Why I Write* series is published
with assistance from the Windham-
Campbell Literature Prizes, which are
administered by the Beinecke Rare
Book and Manuscript Library at Yale
University.

Yale University Press books may be
purchased in quantity for educational,
business, or promotional use.
For information, please e-mail
sales.press@yale.edu (U.S. office) or
sales@yaleup.co.uk (U.K. office).

Copyeditor: Susan Laity

Set in Yale Design type by
Newgen North America.
Printed in the United States of America.

Library of Congress Control
Number: 2021931613
ISBN 978-0-300-25040-4
(hardcover : alk. paper)

A catalogue record for this book is
available from the British Library.

This paper meets the requirements
of ANSI/NISO Z39.48-1992
(Permanence of Paper).

10 9 8 7 6 5 4 3 2 1

OF SOLIDS
AND SURDS

Notes for Noël Sturgeon, Marilyn Hacker,
Josh Lukin, Mia Wolff, Bill Stribling,
and Bob White

§1. "I'm not a writer. . . . The only reason I want to write is because it's the only way I can justify all the other things I didn't do." —Theodore Sturgeon, quoted in Judith Merril, "Theodore Sturgeon," *The Magazine of Fantasy and Science Fiction* (Sept. 1962)

§2. "I think you write sometimes because some people don't have the patience to listen to an older person speak." —Dennis Rickett

§3. I want to write a novel I'd like to read. . . . I write the novel[s] I can't find in my own library or on bookstore shelves. —Samuel R. Delany, Gizmodo

§4. I first said that to myself when I was twenty or twenty-one and had already published five books and was in the midst of yet another; shortly I rewrote it in an early essay. What I remember myself saying was: "I write the books or stories I want to read but can't find on bookstore shelf or paperback book rack." I would have thought something like that had even made it into some early essay or interview, but half an hour online turns up only the Gizmodo version—and an interview I did last year. In the midst of writing my first published book, however, *The Jewels of Aptor* (1962), I realized, one evening when I was trying to be overly modest during an eagerly awaited dinner visit by W. H. Auden and Chester Kallman (it was February 1962), that the book I was in the midst of writing was the most important thing I felt I had undertaken. A little later, when I was still nineteen, I sat in the wood-framed red easy chair my mother-in-law had sent down with a lot of broken china as a house gift for my young wife and me: Marilyn was out at work that day, and I was home. I remember thinking of the various people who, only a few years before, were constantly coming around to my parents' apartment in Morningside Gardens and saying they would be willing to get me a position at a really good-paying job: all I had to do was knock on their office door or give them a phone call and set up an appointment . . . Many had been fairly successful black businessmen who felt it was their responsibility to help out the new generation of young marrieds. I'd also realized it was likely that if I did take them up on any of those offers, I'd have been on my way to a ten-thousand-dollar-a-year job in a decade or so, and ten thousand a year at that time was the equivalent of more than a hundred thousand today. I mumbled to myself loud enough so that somebody might have been able to hear me if they had been in the room with me: "I am never going to make that kind of money. I will be lucky if I make enough to survive."

My first novel was sold a few months later to Ace Books for $1,000; that was also the time when our rent on a four-room apartment in the East Village on the dead-end of East 5th Street was $52 a month, which had been brought down from $58 when the city inspectors had come around and discovered that the landlord was charging $6 over the maximum for a building with that level of plumbing. In short, our rent was $624 a year. Marilyn had a job in which she was making approximately $80 a week as an assistant editor at the paperback publishing company that had accepted my first novel as an anonymous submission. That was a livable wage.

I managed to lose most of the first half of that thousand dollars in a way that I am still too embarrassed to talk about, but within a year, I sold another novel — the first of a trilogy that was completed and contracted for before my twenty-first birthday — and I had learned my lesson about the money I was bringing in.

§5. We lived in that building for four years before we moved to another building, 739 East 6th Street, apartment 4F. One of the objects we had bought first was a wooden four-drawer filing cabinet; it came from a secondhand furniture store two or three blocks away from where we lived, a little to the west and south, and we rolled it back on a convenient dolly that the store loaned us.

When we moved to the new apartment, a block north and east in Alphabet City, it was the first object transported by a helpful neighborhood heroin addict (on another borrowed dolly), who was not more than two years older than I was. A white kid, twenty or twenty-one, he was very proud that he had a good reputation in the neighborhood. He'd been born there and said that too many people knew him for him to be a thief or to break the law in any way other than his heroin habit. Fairly presentable as such people go, he did have the most badly bitten fingernails I think I have ever seen on another human being. I wish I remembered his name. He was a neighborhood character whom we saw on the street many places and whom one regularly said hello to. Once we moved, however, in another year or two, he disappeared from my landscape for ten or eleven years, then turned up again one afternoon in the lobby of the Albert Hotel, where I was staying during one of the periods when Marilyn and I were no longer living together and the number of published science fiction novels had gone up to nine.

§6. It still astonishes me that all nine of those novels and a number of others are still in print and available on my website. Much of that is because, by that time, I'd gotten an extremely good agent, Henry Morrison, whose job (as Henry had explained to me) was not so much to get me big advances but rather to vet my contracts so that my books would continue to make me money once my advance had earned out, which, in most cases, happened pretty rapidly. By 1975, the books were no longer at their initial publisher, Ace Books, but had been taken over by Bantam Books, which was then among the largest and most successful paperback companies in the country. Though today the offspring of Ace still exists, Bantam has been gone for years.

§7. A lot of my writing was done to stimulate myself sexually. That could be a book in itself: A poet whom I greatly respected, W. H. Auden, and whom, as I said above, Marilyn and I invited to dinner in those early years (and who came with his life partner, Chester Kallman [probably because we'd had the sophistication to ask them both]), had written that he found pornography interfered with the aesthetic effect of a narrative. (His rather glib description of pornography, when asked by an interviewer how he would define it, was, "That's easy. It gives me an erection." He himself, however, wrote, I think, a fine pornographic poem, well observed and stimulating enough, I'm sure, at the time it was written, called "The Platonic Blow," which he never owned up to, but it is still available online.) I don't feel that way: I think the erotic response can be worked into the aesthetic response, and I think the entire history of nudes in painting and sculpture is probably proof of this in the classical pictorial and plastic arts. As well, anything written with care can be publishable under your own name. At least once, I tried to lampoon all of this in a book of mine called *Phallos* (2004), which has done moderately well since it was published and is also still available; it was a book that was written to be a kind of footnote to Marguerite Yourcenar's *Memoirs of Hadrian* (1954).

§8. Entailed with the argument above is another answer to the question Why do I write?

Much of my writing has been done because I believed if I understood how and why something worked socially, by narrating the events carefully and clearly, I felt I could show (not tell or explain) how these incidents related to one another and unfolded in the world. I don't know whether that is clear or not, but I think that when one begins to feel that way, however successful one is in achieving it, that is when one becomes a novelist.

§9. Very early on, I wrote because I began to realize (to borrow William Blake's words from *Proverbs of Hell* in *The Marriage of Heaven and Hell* [1790]), "Eternity is in love with the productions of time."

Quickly, as we read, we learn that writing has a relationship with the past. That is where it all comes from, both that which we value and that which we dismiss. To write and publish is to enter a great gambling game in which, in the words of Auden in his 1939 elegy for William Butler Yeats, while there is the probability that with death, or even before, most of it will be forgotten, there is still the possibility that some of us "will become [our] admirers." It is not immortality, but it suggests the closest thing we can have to it, when our works maintain some interest for people beyond our personal death.

Does one write for the future?

I think one has the best chance of future interest if one writes as intensely as possible for the present.

§10. I wrote because it was fun.*

§11. I wrote because, very young, I was terrified by the notion of death.

When I was five or six, I remember sitting on the steps of the embalming room at the back of the chapel in my father's Harlem funeral parlor watching Freddy, my father's embalmer, working on the corpse of a tan woman with reddish hair stretched on her back on the white enamel surgical table with its drain and clamps . . .

"How old is she?" I asked.

"Twenty-eight," Freddy told me, at work in his rubber gloves with the bottles of pink embalming fluid.

"What did she die from?" I asked.

Freddy picked up the tag on the woman's wrist. "Sugar diabetes is what it says here."

"Does everybody have to die?" I asked.

"Eventually." Freddy smiled. "But you won't have to worry about that for a long time . . ."

"But I *will* have to die, won't I . . . ?"

Freddy laughed. "Not for a long, long time . . ."

---

*[CopyEd:] *Change in tense intentional? Or "I write because it is fun"? Previously it has always been "I write."*
[SRD:] Yes, it *is* intentional.

I think his firmness was supposed to be reassuring, but suddenly I felt a dizzying chill. I didn't know what to say or do, but I stood up and said softly, "I'm going upstairs." Halfway back through the funeral chapel, I began to move quickly, and at the stairwell up to the first floor where we lived, I started running. My mother was in the bathroom, scrubbing the floor with a scrub brush. "I'm gonna die!" I burst in, screaming, and threw myself into her arms. "I'm gonna die, Mommy! I'm gonna die!" I think she was bewildered.

"You're not gonna die," she said, as though she took part in half the laugh that Freddy had responded with downstairs.

"No! No! Not now. But I'm *gonna* die . . ."

She pooh-poohed my terror, and for almost forty minutes while I screamed and thrashed and hugged her and sobbed, she tried to find out what was really wrong because she couldn't quite believe that, really, this was all it was. I had seen dozens of corpses before, but it never occurred to me to tell her that it was the reality of a dead body that had initiated my panic.*

---

*[SRD:] This event is recounted in Michael W. Peplow and Robert S. Bravard, *Samuel R. Delany: A Primary and Secondary Bibliography, 1962–1979* (Boston: G. K. Hall, 1980), 8–10. Revised by the author.

But that terror, naked, until I was thirty-five years old would return to me sometimes once or twice a day, eventually every three or four days, and finally, to my astonishment, in my middle thirties, once I had my own child, it vanished—though such attacks are part of the life story of a character, the young philosopher Timothy Hasler, in my novel *The Mad Man* (1994). Every once in a while, in the first years of my teaching, such a panic attack would hit me abruptly, and I learned how to . . . swallow it? . . . not fall down on the floor and have a seizure? And the fact that I could go through these attacks relatively . . . I don't think "calmly" is the word, but it did require saying "excuse me" if I was in front of a classroom when it occurred and, from time to time, going out and getting a drink at a hall water fountain.

For what little it is worth, this chronic condition, which at that time I shared with no one I knew, was the background against which I wrote and published five novels; spent three weeks in a mental hospital for a mild nervous breakdown that I believe stemmed from overwork; produced, scripted, and edited two films and directed another; taught my first term as a visiting professor at SUNY Buffalo as visiting Butler Chair Professor; and also wrote and published three collections of essays on science fiction—*The Jewel-Hinged Jaw, Starboard Wine,* and

The American Shore: Meditations on a Tale of Science Fiction by Thomas M. Disch—"*Angouleme.*" It was not until this infirmity managed to take care of itself that I could actually write about someone who suffered from it in *The Mad Man* (Timothy Hasler), though he is not the main character. If you asked me what the relationship between my writing—fiction and nonfiction—was to this condition, it was a way of not becoming obsessed with it, of letting it take care of itself naturally and not letting it defeat me.★

        †One of the insights that came to me when I got out of Mount Sinai's day-night program in the

---

★[CopyEd:] *I'll say it didn't defeat you—what a list of accomplishments! And what a powerful story this note offers; it goes to the heart of something we all experience at some point or another. This is such a strong paragraph that I would suggest ending note 11 here and moving the following material into note 12. See my next query for more on this.*
[SRD:] STET.

†[CopyEd:] *As noted, I was wondering whether this paragraph and the last line might work better as the opening of note 12 instead of the ending of note 11. In note 11, you discuss your discovery and fear of mortality, and the previous paragraph about not letting that fear defeat you would make a strong ending to the note. What follows here, about refusing to learn to be a mental patient, would make an equally strong opening for note 12, in which you enlarge on the idea.*
[SRD:] No, leave it where it is. These are all habitual panic reactions, which have gotten smaller and smaller over the years but still happen when I see a moving image of someone in a high place, for example, in a film or TV show.

summer of 1964 is that the theories of the psychiatrist* Thomas Szasz about the way someone learns to become a mental patient are remarkably apt. In my high school years, I had befriended a woman named Ana Perez, who did not live at her home but at Hillside Hospital in Queens, at its pavilion for adolescent patients. Ana was a smart and interesting young woman, and I started by feeling sorry for her, so I got in the habit of going to visit her pretty much every week or two.† One of the things I also did

---

*[CopyEd:] *OK to add? I'm sure I'm not the only person who would have to look him up.*

[SRD:] Sure, if you think so. I remember when he was a household name, along with R. D. Laing and, indeed, Freud.

†[SRD:] At one point, the hospital said I couldn't see her anymore because she had become too obsessed with me. Once I was out of her life, she was transferred to a halfway house on St. Marks Place (though I am not sure, I believe it was the building that housed the orphanage where Little Orphan Annie had lived in the comic strip). By this time, Ana had transferred her obsessive feelings onto a youngish male social worker who worked there named Al Hanson, whom I remember coming to see us once at our 6th Street apartment. Ana and I became friends again, and she became the link between Marilyn and a post office worker and his wife, Baird and Margie Robinson. See "Three Seasons, 1944 (*for Baird Robinson*)" in *First Cities: Collected Early Poems, 1960–1979* (2003). It was Marilyn's attempt to narrativize an incident that Baird told her when we all knew each other in the early 1960s. Baird's mother, Rosemary Bruning, once drove Marilyn, myself, and Margie up to her home

almost entirely for her—although it was something I had always wanted to do anyway for myself—was start a singing group, the Harbor Singers. It consisted of myself, David Litwyn, Judy, a black neighbor of mine from my Harlem years, Laura Hunt, and Ana Perez herself. When Judy left to go to Radcliffe as an early admission student, Laura took over for us. At the first rehearsal, we all realized Laura had the best voice of any of the four of us, though Ana came very close and was also an excellent guitarist.

I, too, played guitar.

§12. I began therapy once a week in the sixth or seventh grade at the Northside Center, run by a Doctor Kenneth Clarke. The therapy continued on and off through high school, and beyond. At the same time, I began what soon became weekly or bi-weekly trips to Hillside Hospital, where I met and rather enjoyed the friendship of some of the other kids in the adolescent pavilion with Ana; now that I had actually had my own breakdown and a therapist had suggested that I spend time in the day-night program, I

---

in Brewster, New York. An ex-advertising woman, Rosemary was quite a character. She drove with a paper cup of gin on the dashboard because, she said, if she were pulled over, she knew she would be in serious trouble, so, she claimed, it helped her drive safely.

realized, with my reading of Szasz, that I was simply teaching myself how to be a mental patient and that if I wanted to be a writer, this was not the best way to do it.

§13. I write because somewhere I heard an anecdote about Michelangelo that had the ring of truth: A great Italian baron had been taken with the sculptor's art, sought him out, and, after knowing him for a few days, decided that he was the prince of artists. He had asked to be taken to a tavern where the artists of Florence were supposed to gather and drink in the evening.

Obediently, the artist took him one evening to the tavern. After three evenings at the place, the lord said, "But all I hear among these men is talk of stone and chisels and files, gesso and tempera and pigments. I expected to hear about beauty, the truths that we learn when we gaze up at their works, the perfection that they create for us. Why do they waste their time talking about these trifles?"

Michelangelo answered, "But perfection is the sum of trifles, and perfection, my lord, is no trifle!"

Another tale associated with the artist and architect (who was in love with the boy Tommaso dei Cavalieri, both the model for his *David* and inspiration for his book of sonnets) is that he told the same lord when the lord asked, "How do you know you have a well-composed statue?"

Replied Michelangelo, "You take your statue to the top of a grassy slope, overturn it, and let it roll to the bottom, and if any part breaks off, your statue is guilty of poor composition."

Looking over many of Michelangelo's (not to mention Benvenuto Cellini's or Praxiteles') works, I do not find this story so self-evidently true, and as sculptors move forward into the great moderns, such as Jean Arp and Eva Hesse, we seem to lose the principle entirely. Why, I wondered, though I loved to draw and paint as a child and even make little sculptures from wire and wood, did I seem to move further and further from working in the plastic arts and more and more into writing about them? I loved them, but, young, I soon become terrified of owning them. They seemed far too fragile, and those arts that could be reproduced—the book, the film, the video or audio tape—were the only ones that left me with any certainty, even though I loved the museums consecrated to the creation of individual artists' hands and eyes.

§14. Here's an account of a person who was important to me: a British SF writer—I think it was Josephine Saxton. She invited Marilyn and me and Peter

Nicholls* to visit her in the north of England – she had a large house, was married, and (unknown to Marilyn) was having an affair with Peter.

At least once when we were coming down the steps we looked over the banister and through an open double door in a largely white wall, we saw Peter and Josephine making out on the carpet.

I thought it was funny, but shortly realized that Marilyn was somewhat miffed by it. Probably she thought it was just rude.

Saxton was dark complected – probably darker than I was. I remember her telling us once over coffee that her nickname among her schoolfriends used to be "Nig."

While we were there or after we left, Saxton read an early draft of my novel *Trouble on Triton* (1976).† On finishing, she wrote or phoned me, "But what happened to Lawrence? He was my favorite character!"

Indeed, I had dropped him out of the story shortly after the war. Thus, when I set about revis-

---

*[CopyEd:] *Identify Peter Nicholls?*
[SRD:] Peter Nicholls (1939–2018) was an Australian-born writer and editor of *The Encyclopedia of Science Fiction* (1995), whom Marilyn and I knew in London.
†[CopyEd:] *Suggested because you usually give dates of novels.*
[SRD:] Fine.

ing the novel, I concluded his story arc with the ending it now has: the old man goes on to become a vastly popular eighty-year-old rock star with admiring young groupies who are all over him.

(Fifteen years later, my hundred-year-old aunts were to become their own brand of celebrities — so I seemed to have latched onto something . . .)*

One reason the book is a "heterotopia" is because for Lawrence, Triton could be a utopia, while for Bron it was a place where the pressures of freedom drive him all but mad as he lives out the fantasies and prejudices he has brought with him from Mars — very much a dystopia, as apparently for a while it had been for Ashima Slade.

Many people have liked the novel, but I have not read anyone who analyzed it in this way; though Saxton's suggestion was crucial in helping me to push the book toward its own ideal form.

With an earlier book, *Nova* (1968), back in New York, a friend and mentor, Dick Entin, began with a good suggestion on reading the first draft. He found the ending too benign — the protagonist, Lorq, had emerged unscathed. Dick's metaphor was that I had

---

*[CopyEd:] *I love this aside.*
[SRD:] Thanks.

used a volcano to light a cigarette.* And I agreed—
and rewrote it as the near-tragedy it now is.

Moby-Dick cannot be a story in which Ahab
walks away as free as Ishmael.

Dick made another suggestion—that my vil-
lain, whom he saw as an evil businessman, was simply over the top. Dick had been in business himself,
and while he had no love for the class, he said my
ending was too grand opera. So I took out Prince's
"message," broadcast through the Alkane museum.

Among the first reviews, Algis Budrys's was
spectacular, but he said—so that I would not get a
swollen head—that there was one flaw. What happened to Brian? For him that was a hole in the
story—and of course that had been answered in the
"message," so I decided that my initial feeling had
been correct; for the book club editions, a couple of
months later, I put it back. At least a couple of readers have told me that revelation makes the novel.

Writers do not know everything about their
stories.

Such experiences are what make me feel that
one does not need workshops: too quickly they become, at least by implication, votes and commit-

---

*[CopyEd:] *Marvelous.*

tees — and that's not what is needed to make art. What one needs is one or two readers sensitive to the moral and experiential symmetries and anticipations the work creates in readers' minds — one of whom is the writer.

§15. You can put together more interesting combinations of words in science fiction than you can in any other kind of writing — and they actually mean something. You can say things like "The door dilated" and it's not just a poetic metaphor. When you say, "Her world exploded," you are not just giving a muzzy metaphor for a female character's mental state. You reserve the margin for the words to mean that a planet belonged to a woman and it blew up. So SF is sensually very pleasing to work with, just at the level of language. Also, I think what happens with mundane or naturalistic fiction is that you have characters who succeed or fail in what they try to do, but they succeed or fail against the background of the real world, so their successes are always some form or way of adjusting to the real world, and their failures are always a matter of being defeated by the real world. So in a funny way, the only thing that mundane fiction can talk about is either madness or slavery — people who adjust to the world and therefore are slaves to it, or people who are defeated by the world and are therefore mad because they shouldn't have fought in the first place.

But I do think there's something else to be discussed, other than madness or slavery. In a science fiction story, because success or failure is measured against a fictive world that is itself in dialogue with the real or given world, that dialogue is much more complicated and the resonances are richer for me, and I enjoy working with the harmonies that I can produce. Of course, we all know that there are many things about science fiction that are predictable too. One of the problems — after I've given this glorious and glowing account of all SF's potential — is that for a long time SF has been a kind of marginal writing, a highly conventionalized writing in many ways; so you have a writing situation with many hard and fast conventions; but looked at from another direction, you can do absolutely *anything* in it. When you can do *absolutely* anything, however, what you tend to do is fall back on the conventions.

§16. Back in the early months of 1982, I saw a preview of the movie *Conan the Barbarian,* in which there is a really offensive queer-bashing scene. The entire preview audience hissed. And in the film's plot, which obviously on some level was designed to be an "antisexist" plot, there were so many sexist elements that every time one came by, the audience hissed again.

But that was a time of great change. It was the Upper West Side of New York, a highly liberal area, and it was a time when some audiences, if they were sensitive enough, *would* boo something in a movie preview that was supposed to get their approval.

The other thing probably worth saying is that the bad politics in science fiction come from the same thing that bad politics in most art come from. And it's probably worth noting also that in a number of areas the politics in science fiction are at least a step or two ahead of those in the other arts. I think it's important to remind people again and again — and also to remind the best-intentioned people, because they forget this — that what makes statements like "Blacks are lazy and shiftless," "Women are lousy drivers," or "Homosexuals are emotionally unstable" racist, sexist, or homophobic is not the statements' content, however wrong or ridiculous that content may be. What makes them racist, sexist, and homophobic is the vast statistical preponderance of these particular statements in the general range of utterances of most people most of the time. The fact is, such statistical preponderance makes it almost impossible to say anything else about blacks, women, or gays. It's the silences in the discourse such statements enforce around themselves that give them their ideological contour. And this is why you have to correct the statistical balance. This is what's wrong with people trying to censor such statements, in an attempt to right oppressive wrongs. You don't right the imbalance – the inequality – by suppressing discourse. What you have to do is allow, *encourage* even more: intrude new discourse into the area of silence around these statements and broaden the subject. Then such statements become comments about just one or a few observed individuals, statements that are either right or wrong, silly or interesting.

§17. Here's an old insight that I've offered many times throughout my career, realized as far back as my first novel, which I started in 1961: One of the best ways to portray characters is as a combination of purposeful actions, habitual actions, and gratuitous actions. And somehow even the most insignificant male character almost always gets portrayed as a combination of all three. However, their same writers will find it impossible to portray women characters as exhibiting all three kinds of action. If the woman is an evil woman, she will be all purpose with no habits and nothing gratuitous about her; if she is a good woman, she will be all gratuitous action with no habits and no purpose. It's a strange phenomenon. So when I was writing a set of three books called *The Fall of the Towers,* I sat down and made lists of all three kinds of action for the women characters; then as I got to the end of a chapter I would realize that I hadn't put them in. This habit has all the structure of a psychosis. It really does. When you discover that you are a victim of a psychosis, you realize just how deeply it works into the whole of society.

§18. The work I like to do is most easily done with pen and paper first, yet eventually we learn how to do a fair amount of it with typewriter and paper, and then keyboard and screen; but at each step, we have to learn to do more with the keyboard that involves leaving signs on the screen of where, in a very small, very complicated circuit, we have left the signals that tell us where the text is now lodged.

§19. William Gaddis: *" — My dear fellow, remember Emerson's advice, Basil Valentine said, and paused.

---

*[CopyEd:] *Did the original have quotation marks for Valentine's speech? I have tentatively added single quotation marks, but if they weren't in the original, I'll take them out. Also, I've suggested adding Gaddis's first name because some readers won't know him. It's a wonderful quotation!*
[SRD:] No, it was done European style, with dashes. The quote is from *The Recognitions,* 1955.

There was a crash at the corner. From where they stood they could see that the cab had hit a bus. — We are advised to treat other people as though they were real, he said then, lighting his cigarette, — because, perhaps they are." This is, perhaps, the best solution for solipsism I know. I first found it in Gaddis's *The Recognitions,* which I was lucky enough to encounter the year it was published, at the home of Fradley Garner, a boyfriend of my cousin Barbara's; he was Gaddis's down-the-hall neighbor in Greenwich Village's MacDougal Alley.

§20. I've always seen myself as someone with multiple talents — some nowhere near as good as others but visible when taken in context. For many years, I was not sure whether I was going to be singer or a musician. I felt I was a first-rate arranger until the week of my birthday in 1968. Till then, I'd felt there was equal chance of my giving up writing and going on to music as there was my continuing to devote myself to writing. But now I began the five years of work that took me all over the country and even to England (you can follow my itinerary in the place-date subscriptions to my novels *Dhalgren* and *Triton*) that represented a final turn to writing. In San Francisco, I directed a small super-8 film, *Tiresias,* the single copy of which was lost in the mail.* I directed a play in French. And I returned to New York (twice) and continued writing fiction and wrote and edited three more (short) movies, one in black and white, two in color.

Thus the question "Why do you write?" seems oddly skewed. The only art that I more or less rigorously suppressed — except in moments of private self-indulgence — was poetry. Even then, sometimes I slipped.

§21. Have I directed for the same reason I've written? I'm not sure. Certainly I'm aware that some of the arts require more stamina and focus than I've been able to give them, and as I've grown older and physically weaker, I've certainly given up filmmaking and gone back to writing.

---

*[CopyEd:] *Oy, what a tragedy!*
[SRD:] And about three weeks of my life writing letters to the post office and trying to find it. It was in both color and black and white, had been filmed by a man named Robert Mooney, with both interiors and exteriors, and featured him, his lover Peter Rooney, and Marilyn and myself, and it had been announced in the "about the author section" of one of my novels. Eventually I lost the script as well — whenever I've done films, they've always entailed pretty detailed scripts. I've always suspected if that film had made it into my hands, a whole thread of my life might have been different. Thank you for your kind comment.

Why?

Is that a reasonable way to frame the remainder of my attempt to answer the initial question "Why do you write?" Let's assume it is.

§22. I am still deeply unhappy with the way I speak extemporaneously in public, which is, again, my bow to one of my writing masters, Theodore Sturgeon.

§23. The *Iliad*—the Story of Troy—is a far more complex poem than the *Odyssey*.

It is not so much about a war as about the way the squabbles among the Greek tribes, including Achilles' tribe, the Myrmidons, lead to the destruction of a city at the rim of Asia Minor. The Anger of Achilles, we are told in the invocation, is the topic of a complex tale. And who is Achilles? He is a gay, and possibly transgender, warrior in a tribe that maintains an "army of lovers"* much like the Spartans hundreds of years later, who does not want to fight, but whose honor has been offended by the withholding of a slave girl named Briseis, and he will not

---

*[CopyEd:] *Whose quotation is this?*
[SRD:] It's not a quote and refers to a term derived from a passage in Plato's *Phaedrus*.

fight, he tells his own lover, Patroclus, until she is returned . . .

*When Menelaus sent Odysseus to Achilles to demand he come to Troy and fight alongside the Greeks, Achilles dressed in women's clothing and retired/hid among his women. Somehow Menelaus discovered his female name, and called him out— that name is not told in the tale. But in his book on poetic magic, *The White Goddess,* Robert Graves quotes Sir Thomas Browne's suggestion that, with a little sleuthing, it can be retrieved . . .

In a situation such as a war where no single person could have the big picture, the *Iliad* might have acquired as a nickname "the Greek Squabbles"

---

*[CopyEd:] *The story in this paragraph does not appear in the* Iliad; *it's a later Roman story. According to the main source, the* Achillead, *it was Odysseus (not Menelaus) who found Achilles hiding among the daughters of Lycomedes, and he flushed him out by offering the "women" clothing and jewels with a sword mixed in; when Achilles chose the sword, Odysseus knew he was a man. Unless you mention that he was not at Troy, it looks as though Achilles hid while at Troy, after he was dishonored by Agamemnon. Perhaps rewrite it?*

[SRD:] I'm just assuming that the story is known. When I was growing up, we read versions of these in elementary school, and by the time I was in high school, everyone in our school was reading Graves's *The White Goddess*, and had his two-volume paperback, *The Greek Myths*, as a crib. I'll try to work a little more of it into the sentence.

(rather than the Trojan War). One of its most moving themes is how people who might have seen the larger picture — Cassandra and Laocoön — were tragically ignored and thought to be magicians.

§24. When I was in the sixth(?) grade, I had the great fortune to see the English actor Michael Redgrave (I was taken by my friend Peter Ascoli) in the American performance of Jean Giraudoux's extraordinary antiwar play, *La Guerre de Troie n'aura pas lieu,* in Christopher Fry's elegant translation, *Tiger at the Gates* (1955). It helped make me a pacifist; a paraphrase of the near climactic lines still stays with me: "On the eve of the war, the generals of both sides meet and confer and explain to each other that war would be the absolutely worst thing for both sides — yet all creation knows they'll go to war!"

§25. The *Iliad* and the *Odyssey,* along with French playwrights such as Giraudoux and Jean-Paul Sartre and Jean Anouilh, were passions of my early elementary school days, starting in the sixth and seventh grade. Many years later, probably during the time I lived with Frank Romeo, I came under the influence of some people in New York whose classes I went to for six weeks or so, who had a course in meditation that involved "letting go." There were a man and a woman and an odd dozen of people who would sit around a table in a very sunny room, and we would practice a kind of relaxation therapy in which we would work on *not* wanting anything. The logic was something like this: If you could convince yourself that you did not want a thing, then you would enter the emotional state you would be in if you had it. Although they did not talk about the therapy's Buddhist origins, certainly I recognized it as a basic Buddhist approach to freeing oneself from desire. I didn't stick with it very long, but it was useful, I think, in getting me through some of the trauma that accompanied my relationship with Frank himself, which I have written about in other places—largely on Facebook in my Notes.

Shortly after that, I began to work on my autobiography, *The Motion of Light in Water* (1988, '93, '04), and I found myself flooded with early memories, which I tried to write down. *Motion* basically takes me from childhood through my first trip to Europe, and as I wrote in it, up until then my life had been remarkably chaotic, but now I resolved to be a lot more stable; I was living with my daughter: my life would cease to be interesting and, perhaps, my work would become more interesting. This was the situation I lived in for the next forty years, in the same apartment at 184 West 82nd Street.

This was the case until, finally, I accepted my son-in-law and daughter's invitation to move down to Wynnewood, Pennsylvania, on September 10, 2015.

Over that forty years, such works as *Hogg* (2004), my film *The Orchid* (1971), my novels *The Mad Man*, *Phallos*, and more substantial works such as *Dark Reflections* (2007) and *Through the Valley of the Nest of Spiders* (2012) now materialized, along with the films done to please Frank, *The Aunts* (1984?) and *Bye Bye Love* (1982?).

Here is the place to add: anything that looks as if it's too good to be true, probably is.

§26. Often today, the prospect of writing, especially when it's a matter of answering questions that I have already answered before, strikes me as unbearably exhausting. A week from this particular date (April 29, 2019),* I have been asked to go up to New York City and take part in something that could conceivably be of interest, but because so much of it is a retreading of things that the people who have asked me were inspired by from elements in my work written almost twenty years ago or more,

---

*[SRD:] For the event, see *Frederick Weston & Samuel R. Delany in Conversation* (New York: Visual AIDS, 2021).

right now it doesn't strike me as very interesting. I can only hope that when I get to the venue and talk to the largely younger people who will be involved something will move me to articulation. It entails going to the 42nd Street area and standing in front of sites that have since been torn down and reading from *Times Square Red / Times Square Blue* (1999). The man who is organizing this has picked out the sections, and I have just marked them in a copy of the book that I plan to take with me to read from.

I had an editor friend named David Hartwell, who, indeed, was my best friend in the science fiction community in which I made my living for many years — and who himself, I felt, was an extremely important editor in a field in which the editors proved again and again to be the heroic people who contoured the field's history — and he used to say that in all his years as a professional editor, he never published anything without finding within the first five minutes when it came back from the printer, something that was amiss with the text. For myself, the realities of publication have always offered some kind of disappointment, for much the same reason. The writer often feels like Sisyphus climbing his mountain and rolling his rock uphill, hoping for a book whose print is not too small, and which does not have a major typographical error within the first ten pages. I suppose I write in some sort of blind hope that the book that appears will itself be a wonderful object.

Of course, what we writers get is a mass-reproduced text that, in one way or another, is always inadequate.

§27. Several of my books have grown out of a sense of crisis, a sense of demand from the world: *The Tale of Plagues and Carnivals* (1984), or *The Mad Man*, and even *Atlantis: Three Tales* (1995). This last came not so much from a "crisis," but because I was then fifty years old and I wanted to show what I could do; I put together those three tales very much with Flaubert's *Trois Contes* as my model. Tales two ("Eric, Gwen, and D. H. Lawrence's Esthetic of Unrectified Feeling") and three ("Citre et Trans") are basically — even strictly — autobiographical, though for the third one, set in Greece, I tried to discipline myself to use only incidents that I remembered. But I allowed myself to put them in the most appealing musical order, which I'm pretty sure was not always chronological. That is to say, they are more narrative essays than fiction.

One of the things that was happening when I wrote them was finding myself repeatedly returning to incidents in my recent past and childhood, and I felt as if my mind were giving these up because soon I was not going to be able to remember them anywhere near as well as I could right then, so that I'd better get them down before they vanished.

Atlantis: Model 1924 is a heavily researched short novel about my father's first years in New York. The two-column structure that I come back to again and again is one I had first tried as early as *Babel-17* (1966) and used in my essay "On the Unspeakable."

*From the first, I've often wondered why color illustrations can't be more easily worked into fiction than seems to be the case. Much American color printing is done in Hong Kong because it's cheaper, but that is like wondering why the sky is blue in so much fiction when it's gray so often in these days of climate change and smog. That is to say, the answer to both is probably capitalism, and the shipping costs are still less than the cost of printing it here.

§28. My very first novels were conceived with color decorations. I always liked art and drawing. Probably

---

[CopyEd:] Might this paragraph work better in note 26 instead of here? It doesn't seem to have anything to do with crisis, but it does have to do with some of the ideas about the printed novel that you raise in note 26. The order I'm suggesting then is: note 26 with this paragraph, note 28, note 29, note 27 (minus this paragraph), note 30.
[SRD:] STET.

this is one of the reasons why I have been so enthusiastic about comic books and graphic novels, both in color and in black and white. The fact that the science fiction community tends to be socially far closer to the comics community is because both, for many years, were considered paraliterature, so that if you did one, you were thrown, by the greater forces that be, together with the other. When I was asked to make a film, it's no accident that many of the young actors I was able to commandeer were, indeed, young comic book artists, such as Alan Weiss, Bernie Wrightson, and Frank Brunner, as well as comics writer Mary Skrenes, and some of the opening sections were filmed in Dennis O'Neil's* East 3rd Street apartment. I don't think the denizens of those communities work less hard than any others.

§29. Harold Bloom's answer to the question "Why do writers write?" is fascinating: Artists create in rebellion against the failure to create. There are a number of elementary ways in which that failure can strike them. One is the failure of another artist to tell the truth, to get it right, to make his or her report accurate. Several times this has struck me

---

*[SRD:] Dennis O'Neil (May 3, 1939–June 11, 2020): a well-known comic book editor and writer. See Wiki.

personally, and if the reader can recognize a step forward on the simple measure of truth and accuracy, often the work can gain power because of it.

§30. Only two of my novels started out as specifically experimental and specifically responses to crises. One was a social crisis, and the other was a personal one.

The Tale of Plagues and Carnivals began quite baldly as a response to the AIDS crisis back in 1983 — that is, it grew out of a sense of that crisis. Because of the topicality and urgency of my own undertaking, I felt it was worth the risk to hoist up on my own shaky shoulders the burden of the experimental when I decided to take on AIDS, life, and death in a novel started in 1983 and finished in June of '84.

The judgment of the crisis was *not* that I must reach as many people as possible; rather it was: the people I reach I must reach as intensely as possible. I wanted to create a reading experience at least as intense as the most intense novelistic reading experiences I had had — the ones given me by Harlan Ellison's "Death Bird," Joanna Russ's *The Female Man*, William Faulkner's *The Sound and the Fury*, and Alfred Bester's *The Stars My Destination* (a.k.a. *Tiger, Tiger!*).

My publisher was bewildered by the manuscript—and through a kind of self-fulfilling prophecy, *Flight from Nevèrÿon* (1985), which contained the novel *The Tale of Plagues and Carnivals,* over two printings only sold 85,000 copies. At the time, my other books were selling in the 150,000–250,000 range. I'm still convinced that if my publishers had dared to print the book in the same numbers in which they had printed my others, it would have sold equally well, if not better, but I'm also convinced that among those readers who read it, it got the effect I wanted: AIDS was fixed in their attention as something important, so that when new information arrived it could and would be dealt with, rather than sloughed off and ignored. That was 85,000 readers back when there were only some 8,000 cases of the disease. However local the accomplishment, I felt I had done what I set out to, but to write that book, I said, even if I don't use all of it, I've got to have the full range of the contemporary aesthetic armamentarium from which to choose. Later in the 1980s, Julian Barnes's *Flaubert's Parrot* (1986) benefitted from the same sense of increased readability that came simply from its greater rhetorical range. For many readers, this and Barnes's next book, *A History of the World in 10½ Chapters* (1990), were also a departure from what most readers think of as traditional plot and traditional storytelling.

My book — indeed the entire series of texts in which *The Tale of Plagues and Carnivals* (1984) falls out as the ninth, novel-length tale — was moderately controversial (as half-a-dozen years before, Russ's *The Female Man* had been). Today that controversy is thirty-six years in the past, but my sense from readers is certainly that *The Tale of Plagues and Carnivals* remains the most readable text in the Nevèrÿon series (Return to Nevèrÿon) — if not the most readable I've produced. The strongest motivation behind the experiment was simple: "I've got things to say, and they are too important to fit them within the structures of narrative fiction as usually presented." For such motivation to produce other than chaos, however, it presumes in the writer a history of reading and seeing what can be done outside those structures, of what's to be won by *going* outside.

In June 1993, I completed a short novel, *Atlantis: Model 1924,* which has the distinction of being the most heavily researched novel I ever wrote. That short novel began almost entirely as a critical consideration: James Joyce's *Ulysses,* T. S. Eliot's *Waste Land,* and Ezra Pound's *Cantos* are, for better or worse, among the twentieth century's paradigmatic literary works in English. Each is presumed, as a text, to stand before an all-but-endless intellectual armamentarium that in its range is said to encompass the entire history and tradition of European art, to which these texts are connected by an all-but-endless number of allusions and references. (Today, many people might include Nabokov's *Lolita* or *Pale Fire* with this collection.) In 1993 I decided to write the short novel that became *Atlantis: Model 1924* to see what it felt like to have the experience of writing such a book.

Joyce's novel is organized around Homer's *Odyssey*. In much the same way, I decided to organize mine around Hart Crane's *The Bridge* (1930). In *Ulysses*, Stephen Dedalus's boss at the school, Mr. Deasy, represents an ironic Nestor, a character from Homer's epic; in *Atlantis: Model 1924*, Sam's Raleigh friends Lewey and John represent ironic portrayals of Luis de San Angel and Juan Perez, historical characters who appear in Crane's poem.

Ulysses is packed with allusions. Before I started (and while I was actually) writing, I filled pages and pages with phrases, most of them from books about Crane and studies of the period, to work them into my text.

When a piece is conceived so cerebrally, at a certain point something has to ground it. I was sure the work would be biographical — but where in my own life I would find the particular passage to interrogate, I didn't know.

In 1992 I was invited by the Dark Room, the Harvard University Black Students' Collective, to give a reading for them in Boston — I believe it was in November. That evening I was scheduled to read with a young writer I'd never heard of before, John Keene. Keene read an extraordinary piece about his childhood in St. Louis, among the black middle class of the city. (It was a section from a three-part novella in eighteen chapters [the same number as *Ulysses*], *Annotations*.) Though I grew up in New York, this was a social stratum I knew well — and hearing Keene, I realized that it was the social stratum from which I wanted to mine my own material, in my case from New York City's Harlem and Raleigh, North Carolina. Since its publication in 1995, I've taught *Annotations* several times.

When I returned home the next day to Amherst, I broke out my copy of Crane's *The Bridge* and reread it for perhaps the tenth time in three weeks; but now, as I was going over the closing movement, "Atlantis," something snagged my attention and came together with a memory of a tale my father had told me several times during my adolescence — one that I'd not thought of for years.

The youngest of ten children, Dad had come to New York City when he was seventeen from a small black college campus in Raleigh, North Carolina, St. Augustin's, on which he'd been born. By his own admission, his abiding motivation for the trip was to see New York City's skyscrapers. On his arrival his brother Hubert met him at Grand Central Terminal and took him directly up to Harlem, so Dad's first view of the city, once they came up out of the subway, was pretty disappointing. Still in quest of skyscrapers, at the suggestion of a friend of his brother's a few months on, that spring my father took a walk across the Brooklyn Bridge. What Dad recalled from that walk, more than the view of the city (which, as I'd taken it many times myself, I knew was quite wonderful), was that the Brooklyn side of the bridge was nowhere near as built up as it is today. The highway decanted into farmland, the road running by some cornfields, practically as if (the simile had been my father's) it led back into North Carolina.

My dad was born May 6, 1906. He came to New York in 1923. I envisioned his walk across to Brooklyn and back as occurring toward the end of April or the beginning of May 1924, just before his eighteenth birthday: April 1924 was the month Hart Crane moved into his Brooklyn residence at 110 Columbia Heights with his lover, Emil Opffer, just on the far side of the bridge. And there, in "Atlantis," of which Crane had already written several drafts about his own time on the bridge, were the lines

> Pacific here at time's end, bearing corn, —
> Eyes stammer through the pangs of dust and
> steel. (51–52)

And

> With white escarpments swinging into light,
> Sustained in tears the cities are endowed
> And justified conclament with ripe fields
> Revolving through their harvests in sweet
> torment. (69–72)

Suddenly I was sure as I have ever been of anything that there, within Crane's famously dense lines, nestled references to the same corn and cornfields my dad remembered when he'd told me the story from more than thirty years before, cornfields now gone beneath the concrete of Borough Hall and Brooklyn Heights, even as Crane's own house (once owned by Opffer's father) had, by the time the poet Alfred Corn went to search it out, already been torn down years before. There's an insightful comment by Robert Musil (whose novel *Der Mann* *ohne Eigenschaften* [1932] I'd taught in a modernist novel seminar the previous spring): There's a period between your father's twentieth year and your own twentieth year that you can never fully understand from a historical perspective. You will never understand the first part because you weren't there. You will never understand the second because you were — but without the tools of logic and analysis honed to negotiate it intellectually.*

Suppose, I wondered, on the Saturday before his eighteenth birthday in 1924, my father had gone down to the Brooklyn Bridge, and suppose he had run into Hart Crane (who would have been twenty-four in that year) on the bridge . . .

Somehow all these notions came together for me, with Keene's piece as catalyst. With my notebook full of jottings and quotes that I wanted to work into it, I began writing the text that afternoon.

I dedicated my novella — that is to say, the book it appeared in — to Keene. I think he was rather surprised. But since then, we've become friends.

If the key to the experimental surface of *Plagues of Carnivals* is the social crisis it grew out of, the

---

*[CopyEd:] *This entire argument, with your extraordinary juxtaposition, is riveting.*
[SRD:] Thank you, on my dad's behalf.

key to the experimental surface of *Atlantis* is in the Flaubertian subtitle, *Three Tales.* I had just turned fifty, and I wanted to strut my stuff, show what I could do.

My reason for undertaking this experiment was, however, not for the results (though, I confess, I'm happy enough with them) but rather to see what it *felt* like to be on the inside of such a conscientious writing process. To repeat and expand, *Ulysses* is the paradigmatic art work for our century as Wagner's *Ring* was paradigmatic for the half-century before Joyce. I wanted to know what, subjectively, it felt like to write a text at that level of allusive density, demanding that much research, with those particular organizational constraints, dependent on that particular mode of personal material.

We can all read Joyce and appreciate him as a meticulous observer of the world around him. Still, a lot of people wonder if he did all the things *organizationally* in *Ulysses* that critics are always finding in it, at the level of allusion and structure. Indeed, the question for most of us is, Is it even *possible* for a writer to do all that?

Well, when I started *Atlantis: Model 1924,* that's what I wanted to find out. (My novella is a kind of literary *Kon-Tiki*—you know, *could* the natives actually cross the sea on their handmade raft?) Any observational elegance the piece did or did not display was, for my purposes, secondary. Having finished it, I can answer the question "Is it possible for someone to do all that?" with an unreserved *yes*.

I can answer "Yes," because I tried it myself. It was an interesting, obsessive, and, in many ways, unpleasant experience. (Three years after writing it, while I can remember many of the allusions, I *can't* remember most of them and would have to check my notebooks to confirm the majority, as there were literally hundreds.) And it was a very different experience from the one I've had writing most of my other books. Critically, however, the experience of writing *Atlantis: Model 1924* was invaluable.

The only thing I can say that strikes me as slightly odd about Joyce's enterprise in the light of my own experience is the following:

Atlantis: Model 1924 took me ten months of arduous work. (That's the same amount of time it took me to write *Trouble on Triton,* a book four times as long, far more traditionally structured, and requiring much less labor.) Most of that work, for me as for Joyce at the deposit library in Zurich when he was writing *Ulysses,* meant that I was buried in other books.

The moment I finished *Atlantis: Model 1924,* because of all the research and the organizational work I'd put into it, a nonfiction work on Crane's poem and his times virtually erupted from me, all but spontaneously — subsequently entitled "Atlantis Rose . . ." It's almost the same length, though it took much less time to draft.

Because of what I went through in the writing of *Atlantis,* there's no way I could *not* have written that essay. So — I'm a *little* surprised that, given what Joyce is presumed to have gone through in the writing of *Ulysses,* he has no major nonfiction work either on Dublin at the turn of the century or on the *Odyssey.* * But this just may be a temperamental difference — there's no nonfiction work on the turn-of-the-century Paris from Proust, either . . . though Proust died, of course, *before* he finished his great novel

---

*[SRD:] Unless he considered the book *James Joyce's "Ulysses": A Study* (1930), with which he'd cooperated fully with Stuart Gilbert, to be a joint essay between them on his second novel. It was the first or second trade paperback (Vintage) I purchased, and I bought it thinking I was buying *Ulysses* itself. Not until two years later did I acquire my Modern Library Giant edition of *Ulysses,* first reprinted in this country in 1933 with Judge John M. Woolsey's decision of December 6, 1933, allowing *Ulysses* into the United States. It was a court battle between Random House and the United States, which had declared the book obscene — and when I bought it, the last thing I thought was that any of my own work might someday appear as a Vintage paperback, a division of the same — the selfsame — Random House.

(arguably, Proust's nonfiction work on turn-of-the-century France in general and Paris in particular is scattered *throughout* his great novel), or, once again, it might even be the result of the change in the class structure between what Joyce's novel represents and whatever, at the social level, my novella responds to.

Now the question arises: Are the 112 pages of *Atlantis: Model 1924* in any way, shape, or form "alternative" fiction? The answer, I assume, is a matter of deciding what it might be alternative *to*.

My personal sense is that the conscientious experiment that impelled *Atlantis: Model 1924* makes it feel, at least to me, closer to "alternative fiction" than, say, *Dhalgren,* written twenty years earlier (1973), which, whatever *its* failings, was basically an attempt to write a more or less interesting novel, as I happened to conceive "interesting" at the time.

(But then, the French experimental writer Raymond Roussel [1877–1933]* was not *trying* to write experimental fiction either. He sincerely believed that the homophonic sentences with which he

---

*[CopyEd:] *Life dates essential? They seem intrusive to me. Perhaps delete?*

[SRD:] I think far fewer people will have heard of Raymond Roussel than Thomas Szasz, though perhaps not with this readership. At any rate, I like life dates, especially for people I've heard of before but whose specific dates I can't bring to mind.

began and ended his tales and novels were simply a method for generating more interesting fiction than that which was being written around him — and when you compare his fiction to some of what was being written around him, he was right!)

Ulysses was certainly alternative fiction at the time it was published in book form in 1922. For practically two decades, it was banned in this country and occasioned a famous court battle. Though hindsight makes its canonization seem inevitable, we know it was a long, slow, and gradual process.

Atlantis: Model 1924 was written in 1992 and 1993. By 1997, its most difficult and least accessible section had been included in the *Norton Anthology of African American Literature* — without my knowing about it till it was a fait accompli. To the extent the Norton anthologies represent for some people a certain degree of canonization, *that's* fast enough to make your head spin! (If only for the speed of its acceptance, I suspect it'll be forgotten equally quickly, or remain as the most eccentric and marginal occurrence, of interest only to whoever collects such marginal and eccentric literary experiments.) But all this only suggests once more that the structure of the world to which various practices of writing respond has . . . well, changed.

Once more, I feel obliged to point out that,

however brief my text, the sheer monumentality of the project again marks the conservative aesthetic behind it — to which its inclusion in the Norton only adds its terminal period. Thus, if it *is* "alternative or experimental fiction," it's a pretty conservative and tame experiment. But as I keep reiterating, as a writer that's who I am.

§31. New forms, as we become aware of them, are often exciting to young writers, and from the vantage point of seventy-seven, the period between the first tentative beginnings of Return to Nevèrÿon in London in about 1975 and February 1987, when I finished my series of eleven stories plus novellas and novels,* I'd lived from age thirty-three to age forty-four, a period that, today, I think of as belonging to, if not exactly my youth, then the prime of my writing life. The paraliterary story series had existed for many years, and it had developed its own logic. Though editors were constantly packaging such series as chapters of a novel, anyone who read Catherine L. Moore's Jirel of Joiry series, Robert Heinlein's Future History series, Isaac Asimov's

---

*[CopyEd:] *Is this correct? Down below you refer to this series as a "four-volume" series.*

[SRD:] Yes, the eleven have been collected into four volumes.

Foundation series, or Joanna Russ's Adventures of Alyx series realized that something more interesting was going on. James Gunn articulated it in a major essay on Asimov. Unlike the developmental relation of chapters in a novel, in a story series the solution of story X becomes the problem of story X+1. Fundamentally, this is a self-critical structure, which is constantly inviting the writer to go back and rethink the material in the previous story, to the point of dealing with the same problem from a completely different point of view, or going back in time instead of forward. Even the apparent abandonment of a theme or idea that suddenly no longer seems interesting can be read as a distinct criticism *of* that idea.

And if you are basically a Freudian, as I tend to think of myself, in the same mode as I think of myself as a small "m" marxian, the critical path, as long as the material is human, constantly leads in a phallic direction ("The phallus is the signifier of desire," Lacan; "Desire is repetition," Freud); between the two halves of this parenthetical assertion, we see the play of forces that creates the series as a critical structure.

Between the end of the novel *Neveryóna* and the two novellas in the somewhat shorter novel that make up *Flight from Nevèrÿon*, thematically the series changes direction from a consideration of slavery/

revolution to sexuality/AIDS. The solution to the problems of slavery and revolution become the problems that have to be dealt with at the increased awareness of sexuality that comes with the advent of AIDS. This last is carried out in two ways in *The Tale of Plagues and Carnivals,* which takes place in two cities, New York City during the middle '80s and the ancient city of Kolhari with its upper-class neighborhood that was once called Neveryóna.

§32. Certainly one of the life lessons that came with AIDS was the realization that the rhetoric of sex had to become much less euphemistic, much more specific and direct. Sex neither causes nor transmits AIDS.

A virus — HIV-1 and HIV-2 — causes AIDS, and it is transmitted from an infected man to an uninfected man or woman by means of anal sex. Also it can be transmitted blood to blood by shared needles or, in its early days, by transfusions from improperly tested blood. For a bevy of reasons, it does not spread through any other forms of contact, though it can pass from mothers to children through the placental wall before birth.

Thus, sexual acts from French kissing to cocksucking do *not* transmit the virus, with or without ejaculation. Tales that include "sex" must be told with a specificity at such a level, or, by definition, they are encouraging the ignorance that spreads AIDS. This is hard for a great many people to understand.

This is why much of the narrative literature that deals with social situations where AIDS is a reality and a danger must be written in a language of specificity where confusion *cannot* occur.

When I wrote my novel *The Mad Man,* the obsession with scientific accuracy led me to print in an appendix the Lawrence A. Kingsley, Richard Kaslow, Charles R. Rinaldo, Jr., et alia study of the risk factors for seroconversions in 2,507 HIV-negative gay men, which was published in the British medical journal the *Lancet,* on Saturday, February 14, 1987. But the specifics of what *does* result in seroconversion cannot be talked about unless the writer resorts to highly specific descriptions of very specific sexual acts.

For me as a writer, this forced me to break precedence and even laws and become what many people could only describe as a "pornographer." Nevertheless, I thought the choice was to do so or to indulge in a general mystification that was tantamount to encouraging murder.

Another way of saying this is that one reason I write is to tell the truth.

§33. One of my most frequently anthologized short stories is the early tale "Aye, and Gomorrah" (September 1966), based on an idea I'd had for some months previously but only drafted in Milford, Pennsylvania, while I was attending the Milford Science Fiction Writers Conference during that month, after attending my first world Science Fiction Convention over the previous Labor Day weekend, out in Cleveland, Ohio.

An irony of the conference is that the idea for the Milford Conference had been based, in part, by the conference founders Damon Knight, Judith Merril, and James Blish a dozen-odd years before, on what they had read of the Bread Loaf Writers' Conference, held in the summers at Middlebury, Vermont. As far as I know, I am probably the sole writer to have attended both: I'd gone as a work-study student on a waiters' scholarship to Middlebury for the 1960 summer session. (You can read about that in my book *Times Square Red / Times Square Blue*.) An early idea behind the story itself was to provide a narrative home for the retelling of an off-color joke that I always had a great deal of fondness for as a gay man. A young man with whom I was sexually involved named Bobby Folsom recounted the joke from someone from whom he'd heard it in jail during a two-year sentence he'd just finished serving in

Florida when my wife and I met him. The gist of the joke was that a tough guy learns that another man is a homosexual, accuses him of it, and threatens to beat him up, and the other man turns around and responds: "Hey, there are two things I really go for, one is sucking on a good cock—and the other is a *real* good fight!" and doubles up his fist. Somewhere that joke is buried in the story, told not about homosexuality but about the "new" perversion invented for the tale, the "free-fall sexual displacement complex." The people who seem to like the story seem to recognize a certain impossibility of satisfaction— or, more accurately, a temporariness to the satisfaction—of any desire as distinguished (so clearly by Lacan) from demand or need.

The tale was also a try at writing the kind of scene that might occur between a gay man and a hustler that on the surface, because of the science fictional distortion, appeared to be occurring between a man and a woman.

And, of course, it was an attempt to use some of my experiences during a ten-day hitchhiking trip with a friend named Jerry Mulqueen to Istanbul, during which Jerry, while he was happy to take the trip with me, knowing full well my own sexual proclivities, was still very uneasy with the idea of going to see a gay friend, John, I had known on a brief acquaintanceship when he had stayed at the home of DeLyse Robinson in her small, picturesque stone house in Anafiotika on a two-week visit earlier that same summer in the neighborhood above the Plaka, on the back of the Acropolis in Athens: a visit which produced my story "Citre et Trans," in *Atlantis: Three Tales.*

§34. The attraction of work—*Through the Valley of the Nest of Spiders:*

For me, the appetites have always been focuses for fiction, and these include food, sex, affection, shelter, and work in general, as well as the abstraction from it of pure pattern that grounds the appetite for art.

In a number of books, which I started writing in all honesty before I wrote anything else, the desire for love, warmth, and sex was a topic, along with the sexualization of the various forces that now and again seemed to prevent their achievement. This might be seen as getting its first specific exploration in Return to Nevèrÿon. The original question I saw myself asking was the paradoxical one: Imagine slaves fighting for their freedom. Now imagine someone with a sexual fetish for the accoutrements of slavery itself: the whips, the chains, or, in the case of the inhabitants of the land of Nevèrÿon, the iron slave collars that identified the actual slave as distinct from the beating marks that might be found on any criminal whether he or she started out as free or owned.

The specificity that the advent of AIDS brought to this argument first manifested itself in *The Tale of Fog and Granite* (1984); this, of course, was two years after AIDS got its acronym: I first saw it applied to the death of an extraordinarily talented young dramaturge who went by the name of Hibiscus (George Harris III), who for several years, first with the Coquettes, then with the Angels of Light and in a number of unconnected shows, was one of the most potent forces in American theatrical production, as he urged actors around him to "hear love's magic music, let the animal in [themselves] flow, and live with the angels of light." I was very lucky to have George's younger brother, Walter, as the star in the twin parts of Ratlet and Androcles in my two-hour radio play *The Star Pit*, which we recorded and edited in late November 1967, and broadcast annually for more than a decade. I believe it was a day or two before Thanksgiving.

Even that play, based on my novella of the same name, was an attempt to present an image of a fluid and flexible group commune. One of its axes was the sexual. The print publication of the text had been one of the first cases in which, minor as it was, I'd ever had any editorial tampering to speak of, and my response had been pretty over the mark.

In the play version, that tampering was removed, and I was very happy with the results. The fine young director-actor Daniel Landau caught the thrust of the material as well as anyone possibly could. The fact that several years later, Danny, whom I had first met as a student at the Bronx High School of Science, died of AIDS fueled some of my personal sense of crisis in my AIDS novel, *The Tale of Plagues and Carnivals*.

§35. "Why did you write *Dark Reflections*?" A number of the reasons I can actually grasp in language. By that time, I was both a fairly successful writer, by my own standards, and a fairly well-established full professor of English and creative writing at Temple University; but I'd also had a fair amount of experience teaching creative writing workshops not only at Temple but at the Clarion Science Fiction Writers' Workshop;* as well I had been an outside member on a number of creative writing dissertation

---

*[CopyEd:] *Clarion Science Fiction and Fantasy Writers' Workshop, as it is now, or did the name change?*
[SRD:] Yes, it did. I'm not sure of the date the name expanded.

committees at the University of Massachusetts and other universities by then. Two facts that one learns from time are, first, that the majority of students who take any college creative writing workshop do not go on to become writers and, second, among those who do, seldom are any what one might call "successful" writers. The life of someone who commits him- or herself to art, by and large, is going to be a life of poverty and second jobs and precious little recognition, even if you stick to it. (Richard Howard has put it succinctly: "To be a poet at twenty is to be twenty; to be a poet at forty is to be a poet." And the sad truth about the second half of this is that to be a poet at forty is not necessarily to be a well-known one.) One of the reasons I wrote the book was to create a fictional text that would show my students the sort of impoverished life that actually awaited them. I was lucky in that I wrote prose that had developed a readership. (I belonged to the category that is considered by most publishers the opposite of commercial: a midlist writer. While sometimes midlist prose writers break out and eventually become successful, most of us do not. I had been extremely lucky with the response to a book called *Dhalgren*.)

The main character in *Dark Reflections*, Arnold Hawley, is, first, a black poet, not a black prose writer, and though he has had several books published, he has rather steadfastly refused to rely on any community of poets for support, though he teaches on Staten Island (in a fictional university) and lives on the Lower East Side. By the 1980s, the Lower East Side had become the East Village because it was notably cheaper than the West Village—and for Arnold not to mix in with this community (which was largely white) was very rare. It had to do with Arnold's aesthetic, however. But he is more enamored of Howard and Hacker than he is of Ginsberg, Waldman, and Berrigan, and he is not at all interested in supporting that which he feels is anything other than first rate. His eighth book won a prize, which is the closest he has ever come to success, but it was not a Pulitzer or a National Book Award or one that was known well enough to garner even the smallest of newspaper mentions.

Hawley is also gay and painfully literate in traditions of poetry that are not the ones that, during the time the book takes place—the years before and just after the turn of the twenty-first century—the young writers who fill writers' workshops are likely to be interested in. He is an overweight black man who eventually must go into adjunct teaching and even then often has to subsist on scrambled eggs and oatmeal. He has attitudes toward art, language, and even life (as well as an extremely impoverished sex life) that he tries to impart to his students, who are not creative writers but simply the young men and women, many of them black, who make up the first- and second-year students in a state university and who are not interested in the kinds of things that fascinate him.

Propinquity has left him as an observer of a number of historical changes, such as the clientele of the Stonewall Inn a year before the Stonewall riots and the changeover in 1968 between the word Negro and the word black, but he has little success in explaining to his students what the significance of these changes was as he observed them, especially thirty years later. The other difference I was trying to portray was the life of a black writer who was, in many ways, different from myself but also black and gay.

After *Dhalgren,* arguably my most successful book, was a nonfiction study called *Times Square Red / Times Square Blue* (1999), which recently went into a twentieth-anniversary edition. If there is a single book of mine that Arnold Hawley could *not* have written, this is it, and its existence earmarks most sharply the difference between Hawley and me.

I think it is interesting, if not painfully ironic, that the first *Publishers Weekly* review of *Dark*

Reflections took upon itself to state baldly that *Dark Reflections* was a Delany autobiography, which is simply ludicrous and, frankly, racist because it assumes that if a black writer writes a book about a black character, he must be writing about himself, or that, indeed, there is only one kind of black writer who can have the valuation of art that Hawley has.

I think that the heuristic thrust of Hawley's portrait is as relevant to the lives of white poets as it is to black ones. The happenstance that it includes a scene that took place in the Stonewall Inn, which Arnold visits the summer before the riots with two gay black friends, probably helped the book take a Stonewall Book Award for 2008. I remember what Michael Cunningham wrote on his winning the Pulitzer Prize for Fiction for his novel *The Hours* (1998): "They waited until I wrote a novel where nobody gave anyone else a blowjob before they gave me the prize."* There is only one blowjob in *Dark Reflections*, and I think most readers will probably assume it is not the most satisfying one in the world, whether they are straight or gay. It's not one you will find in *Times Square Red / Times Square Blue*.

---

*[CopyEd:] *What a priceless assessment!*

§36. Though it speaks of sophistry, I have always liked this argument for atheism:

Atheist: "You don't believe in the Greek god Zeus, who is the mightiest of all the gods, do you?"

Christian: "No, of course not."

Atheist: "And you don't believe in Venus, the goddess of love?"

Christian: "No, I don't."

Atheist: "And you don't believe in Apollo, the god of the sun, or Selena, goddess of the moon, or Poseidon or Hermes or Athena or any of the others?"

Christian: "No. Of course not."

Atheist: "Well, neither do we. And we just believe in one less god than you do."

Despite the cleverness of the argument above, I believe that if there were a god, it would have to be such a complex entity that for a human being even to say that he or she "believed" in it would be tantamount to an ant saying that it believed in the black hole at the center of our galaxy. The ant simply doesn't have a brain large enough to conceive of a galaxy, or its center, or a black hole. It is sheer arrogance, mere hubris for human beings to say they believe in something they call a god when they are precisely the people who are incapable of believing that other people are human and have the same wants and fears and desires and needs as they do, as soon as those people begin to appear the least little bit different culturally from themselves

My spiritual energy goes into believing in the humanity of all of my fellow folk on the planet and the importance of my very distant cousins, such as grass, oaks, mushrooms, not to mention fish, bats, dogs, and birds, of what lives within my horizon and what lives beyond it.

§37. The poet Paul Valéry said that a work of art can never be finished; it can only be abandoned. One reason for this is that as a writer comes back and comes back to the novel or the painting or the poem, it changes under the correction process— and so does the artist. Knowing when to abandon it is what might be called "artistic maturity." A story that almost parodies this process is Balzac's "The Unknown Masterpiece." I have often thought it is my own failing that every time I pick up an old piece of mine and reread it, I still want to make changes.

§38. Before he began the poem for his music-drama *Tristan und Isolde,* Wagner claimed that because neither he nor probably any other human being had ever known perfect and total love, he wanted to write a complex portrayal of such love in a musical theater work.

Again and again, I have found myself drawn to similar projects in fiction, most frequently in novels such as *The Mad Man, Hogg,* and *Through the Valley of the Nest of Spiders,* and even in *Stars in My Pocket Like Grains of Sand.* One cannot know how close someone comes to succeeding in what is finally a highly ironized undertaking of the pursuit of a romantic absolute. Yet I find myself drawn to it again and again, even as I find myself, in Lacan's soundbite, desiring the desire of the other.

In the course of this, it is easy to feel that one has gone astray or been confused or hideously mistaken; yet one keeps returning to the Freudian postulate: repetition itself is desire.

§39. I write because I didn't go into music, and it is much, much harder to revise musical pieces than to revise prose or even oil paintings. I write because I didn't go into dance or film, and the way both of those tend to fall out, they are collaborative arts. One of my favorite filmmakers is Busby Berkeley, and the kind of fantasies he created is what, when I've been lucky enough to be able to make a film with a dozen-odd actors or so, I've aspired to do, such as in *The Orchid.*

I've always had problems following through on things that required physical exertion or more than one person. Probably that's why I never pursued filmmaking to the point where I could create a major narrative, a major dance number.

I understand what editing is about, but that is all behind me. I used to hate Hermes Pan's dance numbers because they always seemed so unimaginatively filmed. He was certainly imaginative and a good choreographer, but when his films were coming out, it was hard for me to separate the filming from the dancing per se.

One of the reasons I liked Cyd Charisse was because she was willing to give up her turnout in ballet numbers in order to look more natural. Michael Parker's films, such as *The Red Shoes* with Moira Shearer and Robert Helpmann, spoke to me a lot, and when the Old Vic brought Helpmann's production of *A Midsummer Night's Dream* to the old Metropolitan Opera House in New York City, with its famously shallow stage — one of the reasons they pulled the building down and built the much deeper stage at Lincoln Center — it all but convinced me to create an Oberon costume complete with wire wings glued over with glitter, where the imagined wing surfaces were completely transparent — which I believe was how they'd worked on the Met stage. My parents and I watched it from a side balcony seat. Indeed, it may have been a box.

The entire company, led by Helpmann and Shearer, *flew* off the stage at the end, leaving a wingless all-but-nude Puck to run to the front of the stage and declaim the epilogue. I still tear up at the memory of his reaching out to the audience: "Give me your hands if we be friends / and Robin will restore amends."

I was not yet ten. I never wanted to be Titania, but I did want to be Oberon or—even before that— Peter Pan . . . or the trickster Puck.

§40. Writing gives me an opportunity to describe and analyze the workings of modern technologies on the lives of ordinary people. It's my opinion that most of us die because of our interaction with one technology or another. My father died at fifty-four, when I was nineteen, of lung cancer: he smoked four packs a day and lived in a fog of formaldehyde, which is an even stronger carcinogen than tobacco smoke. My partner Dennis's father also died at age fifty-four; he, too, smoked and drank; so did his mother. Dennis's father came looking for him one evening and was apparently drunk and wandered out into the street, where he was hit by a garbage truck.

These are deaths that fall out directly from the technologies. My family's good friend Mrs. Ann Jackson, our downstairs neighbor, was a small black woman who, in order to breathe in her last years, had to carry around a container of oxygen. She lived by herself and one day was coming home, apparently trying to change her oxygen, only to discover that she did not have another. The door closed, and she turned around, trying to get out of the house again, and died on the floor in front of her locked door. She was ninety-six. A change in any number of factors, from a caretaker or roommate who lived with her to an extra tank of oxygen might have extended her life by several years.

I feel as though I have become extremely dependent on the kind and skillful people who help me, including my partner and my assistant, but at the same time I am aware that I lack all sorts of abilities that seem to get worse because of increasing short-term forgetfulness and the failure to be able to create new habits in under six weeks. Something as simple as keeping two pill cases stocked with six nighttime pills and eight daytime pills has become a biweekly task that I do not think at this point I could accomplish by myself—or at least it would take substantially longer than it does with my assistant to help, who does not have my short-term memory failings.

Those failures of memory have already made it extremely difficult to continue writing fiction.

§41. "Truth" and "Ideology":

As a gay man who, very young, came to the conclusion that the sociopolitical problems of women were the most important political problems we had to deal with in the world, and all other problems could be read as stemming from those, I find myself in the current moment drawn to or toward a number of positions. I would like to see a woman become president of the country. I would like to see us have an openly gay president.* I have read a fair amount of information that suggests that at least one of our presidents — Abraham Lincoln — was indeed gay or bisexual. (There is at least as much or more circumstantial evidence that Lincoln was gay as there is of the much more easily accepted proposal that Shakespeare was: Shakespeare worked and was fairly successful in a business where many of his fellow actors were, by temperament, transvestites, if not what we might call transgendered. And

---

*[CopyEd:] *We're getting closer to both of those goals!*

nightly, during Lincoln's White House tenure, Captain David Derickson was Lincoln's bodyguard and bed companion; as well, there was his earlier relationship in Illinois with Joshua Fry Speed.) We currently have an openly gay and partnered presidential Democratic contender, Mayor Pete Buttigieg. Yes, this pleases me because it is not contested by the social machinery that used to say it would be better for everybody if it were not so.

I also acknowledge that I would like to see someone like Representative Alexandria Ocasio-Cortez eventually run for president the way Mayor Pete is currently doing, and I find myself writing, as I am now, in the hope that just naming the situation might help it to occur. But I am also aware of the social problems entailed, which can be summed up by a comment John, a long-time housemate of Dennis and mine, once made as to why it was highly unlikely that Hillary Clinton would win her chance at the presidency: "She pees sitting down." In neither my case nor John's does this* represent any sort

---

*[SRD:] I wanted her to win (and so did John), but because I was traveling a lot that year and talking to strangers in airports, I felt it was likely that Trump would win. (As did Michael Moore.) And he did.

of secret wish. (John is as straight as I am gay.) On the contrary, it has to do with an acknowledgment of the sad attraction an overwhelming number of American voters positioned so that the current fiasco of the Electoral College was able to create the disastrous 2016 win for Donald Trump. Apparently, they felt that his assertions, such as "Grab 'em by the pussy. You can do anything" and "I could stand in the middle of 5th Avenue and shoot somebody and I wouldn't lose voters," were an attractive honesty and acceptable transgression.

§42. Among the three writers I felt the closest to — Roger Zelazny (1937 – 1995), Joanna Russ (1937 – 2011), and Thomas M. Disch (1940 – 2008) — Disch and I, while we both lived in New York City, had the closest personal friendship, at least until I began to teach at the University of Massachusetts, and Russ and I had the next closest, which manifested itself in a large collection of letters currently on store at Yale's Beinecke Library. At least once, Russ wrote that she felt her own writing had to be oppositional in order to be worthwhile, and I think I absorbed much of this.

When I look at things that have changed, I am surprised at how little change I see in fashion and music: the range of colors in cars has gone way down so that the vast majority are black, white, or gray, with a few silver or gold suggesting a moment of variation in the boredom along the road. Most men are content with Bermuda shorts as, in the temperate latitudes, we drift into late spring. But there is very little variation in male or female fashion.

Recently, a long-time friend of mine, Njihia Mbitiru, who lives in Nairobi, Kenya, sent me a story to criticize, in which I could not see any of the characters because none of the characters existed as physical beings. I am not sure if this was done consciously in hopes of selling it to an American magazine so that no one would know that the characters were Africans in the future, or if, because they were all Africans, there was no need to differentiate them. There are certainly white people in Nairobi, but the question is, How important are they likely to be in the future? Can fiction talk across cultural lines? Would a narrative in some earth language be even comprehensible if translated into some extraterrestrial tongue — assuming this particular species spoke with its tongue (or tongues) at all? This is a question that has impelled me to write certain sections of my science fiction novels.

§43. I have certainly written simply to play with the language. The creation of sound patterns is evident in the concluding chapter of *The Fall of the Towers* and here and again in *Dhalgren.*

I believe it was Oscar Wilde who first wrote, "The more characterization an author employs, the more his characters come to sound like everybody else." It is first impressions and significant details that distinguish fictive characters, and hunting them up in order to create my own characters for many years was fun. One is always afraid, however, that repetition will undercut the enterprise, especially once readers notice it, which has happened to me on a number of occasions.

§44. Famously, Dr. Johnson said, "No man but a blockhead ever wrote, except for money." Sometimes, apparently, I have been a blockhead. I am writing this collection of anecdotes and repeated borrowings because I am going to be paid for it. There is the hope that by assembling them all I might possibly learn something I didn't know through their assembling or juxtaposition, but I at this point I am not sure what that might be, and I find it more of a chore than a pleasure. Primarily it provides a way to get away from what I already know in Richard Woolf YouTube talks on socialism and losing my way among them, doing the unpaid housework and whiling away time until my assistant gets here to accompany me to a neurology exam at 2:30 down at Jefferson Hospital.

§45. I have written for much the same reason I have taught: to help expose others to works that have given me pleasure, whether Flaubert's *Sentimental Education* or Alan Moore and Eddy Campbell's *From Hell*, Willa Cather's *A Lost Lady* or Richard Hughes's *A High Wind in Jamaica*, or the progression of Junot Díaz's stories in his debut collection *Drown* or Roger Zelazny's ten strongest early long stories, on which his reputation as a serious writer was based, as they are collected in my anthology *The Magic (October 1961 – October 1967)*, along with his earliest novels . . . *And Call me Conrad, Isle of the Dead*, and some others that slid in among his lighter-weight Amber chronicles. By the same token I have written to expose what I have assumed is the failure to think carefully through the material in a novel of ideas, such as Ursula K. Le Guin's *The Dispossessed*, in my extended reading of the text against my own experience, in "To Read *The Dispossessed*."

§46. I believe for a piece of this kind to be useful, it must think against itself, if it is to be other than a citation of texts once completed and the citations of what, for most writers, is self-evident for clarity and generosity* with the hope that a return to the examples can clarify what the process of intelligent attention might yield where things of even more pleasure or use are to be recognized, possibly by others whose cultural orientation is both congruent enough and aslant enough to produce an interesting parallax.

There are as many reasons to write as there are experiences for readers to recognize from a piece of writing. Nor is there any way that the two — writers' and readers'— can ever be wholly congruent.

§47. I don't know. Possibly an ending to come after further expansion?

Isak Dinesen's sideways comment on the problem is one that I am often drawn to: "Every day I try to write a little with neither hope nor despair . . ."

§48. One of the reasons I want to write is to reveal secrets about the past, to tell the truth about the present.

---

*[CopyEd:] *Sorry, I'm not sure what you mean by "citations of what, for most writers, is the self-evident purposes to clarity and generosity." Could you clarify?*

[SRD:] At this point, neither am I. But I'll stand with Browning on "Sordello" on this one: When I wrote it, only God and I knew what it meant. Now, only God knows.

I was aware of the way these ancient stories had traveled through theaters very different from the ones we have today, from theaters in which the groundlings stood and the upper class sat in relatively low balconies, to the prosceniums represented by the old Metropolitan Opera House, where I saw Moira Shearer in a spectacularly engineered *Midsummer Night's Dream* that urged me to memorize most of the play. The words Shakespeare imagined might be spoken by Theseus and Hippolyta, much less the fairy court of Oberon and Titania, convinced me at that point that messages written down and hidden, even if they were not incised in stone with mallets and chisels, might endure for centuries or even thousands of years.

Once, I wrote a message on a piece of shirt cardboard—I do not remember what it said—and slipped it between the door and the jamb of the pocket door that separated my parents' bedroom from my sister's and my bedroom at the front of our house, when we lived only on the second floor and my father's sister, my aunt Laura, and her three children lived on the third floor above us. My house had been there before I was born. I had no reason to think it wouldn't be there many years after I died. Maybe when they did eventually tear down that building in three or four hundred years, maybe they would find the message that a little boy had written. That was an exciting thing to contemplate.

Because of books I had, such as *My Book House,* I had pictures to look at that told the tale of the *Odyssey* and the Homeric mock-epic *The Battle of the Frogs and the Mice.* These also included pictures of traveling Mummers' wagons that inspired the boy Shakespeare to become a playwright and stake his talent in writing tales such as *Coriolanus* and *Titus Andronicus, Antony and Cleopatra* and *Julius Caesar* for the London theaters, such as the Globe and Blackfriars. Shakespeare seemed to know or to be able to invent plausible things that such historical characters might say. Wouldn't people be excited to hear something someone such as I had said before I even knew how to do any writing?

Why couldn't I?

Less than twenty years later, on my first trip to Greece when I was twenty-three, among the places I enjoyed going most in Athens were the sites that bore Hadrian's name: the Tower of the Winds, Hadrian's Library, and Hadrian's Gate. Near the gate, or more probably near the tower, was a stretch of mosaic on the ground around it with square pieces of green tiling, perhaps a quarter of an inch by a quarter of an inch. One of them had come loose, and so I bent down, picked it up, and put it in my pocket. Later that evening, I transferred it to the string and pick compartment of my guitar case, and it eventually came home with me to New York City. When I got my butcher-block desk, it went into the middle desk drawer, in the little compartment where I put things like the original piece of driftglass* and my collection of subway tokens that went back to the very first ones that had been used in New York. Most of those things eventually vanished, but I liked the idea of having a piece of Hadrian's mosaic, as I assumed it to be, that, for all I knew, the second-century Roman emperor had walked on himself if not chosen the color for. As far as I know, that is the only time I was disrespectful to an archaeological site. As well, probably others had laid down new tiling several times since the second century; but in my mind there is a direct connection between those Hadrianic monuments in Athens and my novel of Hadrian and Antinous, *Phallos*. There are no scenes in Athens, but Hadrian clearly has a Greek education from the city

---

*[CopyEd:] *What is "original" about this piece of driftglass? Was it the first you collected? the one that inspired your novel?*

[SRD:] I had already coined the word with a short story, "Driftglass," first published in 1967, before I had ever seen any. I just figured out that logically it must exist. A decade later, Jean Mark Gawron, a young novelist and housemate, brought home a piece from the beach — despite the story, the first piece I'd ever actually seen.

of which he was archon between 125 and 129 C.E. Sadly, I never worked the Tower, the Gate, or the Library into the novel itself, which takes place mostly in Hermopolis — on the border between Upper and Lower Egypt — and concerns the death of Antinous and its aftermath. With research, I had been able to come up with a reasonable story and reasonable dialogue that might have been uttered by the characters in the Adriatic drama of one of the fascinating Roman emperors, who had already inspired writers to tell his tale.

§49: I write because certain aspects of writing are difficult — and, as Yeats said, the fascination with what's difficult has dried the sap out of my veins, and rent spontaneous joy and natural content out of my heart, which is another way of saying it keeps me calm in a world where there are often things to get upset over.

§50: As my late friend Thomas Disch said: Writers would not write if they did not want to be objects of interest. And writing is a way to be interesting.

§51: I write because I am drawn to making verbal structures that superficially resemble others I have made in the past: "Shadows," "Shadow and Ash,"

"Times Square Red," "Some Remarks on Narrative and Technology" . . .

§52: I write because I am and have always been drawn to see capitalism, at least in the form we know it, overthrown, and yet at the same time, because I know that it is "easier to imagine the end of the world than it is to imagine the end of capitalism," I am also drawn to make as much money as I can for my partner Dennis, who, other than having been brought up to accept black people and brown people as friends of his English, Irish, German, and generally alcoholic family, was given little political education and precious little formal education at all until he spent six years on the street, where his panhandling and bookselling allowed him to go to the occasional dirty movie on 42nd Street, as I did (we both frequented the same theater, only at different times, so that we never met there), and he decided I was safe enough to spend a weekend with at the Skyline Motel on West 51st Street, at 10th Avenue, and to visit in Amherst, Massachusetts, and to share my bedroom at 184 West 82nd Street, as talked about in my graphic novel *Bread & Wine,* and in the texts comprising *Letters from Amherst,* once we did meet on 72nd Street, just east of Broadway in 1990 or 1991.

§53: I am drawn to write because, within the strictures of an unusual academic life, plagued by dyslexia (I became a full professor without completing a year of college), and without a pension fund at the time I retired (which was certainly due to the dyslexia and the AADD that accompanied it), I want to live as comfortably as possible, which now includes a four-room apartment in the Fairmount* of Philadelphia, an assistant, who is a former student whom, when he applied for the job, I didn't even remember from my class, though others from that class had made an impression.

My current feeling is that I cannot write fiction, save the hardest-won short pieces, and I manage to turn out some nonfiction largely because of my history — and it is, indeed, that history and my memories of that history that alone constitute the "I" I happen to be, who is more and more dependent on friends, here and there, and on family.

I write because I have an agent, who is a little older than I am, and whom I have had throughout my life, without ever changing, and because I

---

*[CopyEd:] *Is this a neighborhood?*
[SRD:] Yes. It's also known as the Museum Neighborhood, and contains the Philadelphia Art Museum, the Rodin Museum, and the Barnes Collection, all within walking distance, on a good day.

have an editor and literary executor, who is involved in the overwhelming job of editing my journals, though he is currently discommoded by a beaver who has interrupted the process for a few days in a landscape that, politically, is not the same as it was twenty years ago, since the last time the same problem came up, the state had enough to move beavers to different habitats, whereas today they must be killed outright—a situation that does not make my literary editor-executor (with whom, for years now, I have only talked by phone and email, and occasionally snail mail) very happy.

§54: I write because the first executor I had, a very good friend and all-purpose general problem solver, Robert Morales (1958–2013), was someone I met when he was seventeen, on the same day that I met an artist named Mia Wolff, who was nineteen, and who, together and apart, continued as very good friends up through his death of undiagnosed colon cancer at age fifty-four, eight years ago.*

---

*[CopyEd:] *You write because your first executor was someone you met when he was seventeen? That, syntactically, is what this says.*
[SRD:] Yes, though he didn't become my executor till twenty-five or thirty years later.

§55: When I write, I am as much the person who makes the mistake as I am the one who corrects it when I rewrite. I am as much the person who gets to the place in a sentence or a paragraph where I realize I am ignorant of a date or the name of a city where some historical event occurred as I am the person who, twenty minutes later, returns from the encyclopedia on the lower library shelf or turns from the computer screen after a ten-minute Google hunt to fill it in. Writing above a certain level requires, however, that you gain some understanding of both, not only within your "self" but out in the world. Perhaps this is what has given me a career-long fascination with people who cannot speak or write at all, as well as an equal fascination with poets (which etymologically means "makers" and more recently "makers of things from language"), though the "self" I present to the world is neither one nor the other, thanks to the Other that is always there in me, the "I" that "I" am always struggling to overcome. This is the only way I can resolve the aporia (the contradiction; and *aporia* was Plato's word, after all) as to why Plato, who was such a fine writer in the Greek of his time, in his hypothetical and optative society so famously excluded the poets from his Republic. (The optative is a Greek grammatical mood, similar to the subjunctive, from which we get the word *options*.) Plato wanted the

poets who were there to be better than they were—
that is, to choose the option to be more faithful to the
idea of truth, which, when talking about an imagined
world, is not quite the same as actually banishing
them from the actual. I am not suggesting, as some
folks have, that Plato wrote science fictions. But *I*
do. That helps me read him—as, doubtless, having
written one novel himself (*Marius the Epicurean, His
Sensations and Ideas* [1885], a favorite of both Virginia
Woolf and James Joyce) and started another (*Gaston
de la Tour*) helped Walter Pater, seven years later, in
his wonderful *Plato and Platonism* (1893), have the
insights about the philosopher he did. Far closer to
our day than to Plato's, Pater noted that, had he been
writing in ours, Plato could have been a great novelist. The ten-volume set of Pater's complete works—
which her father had not allowed in their library
when he was alive—was among the first books Woolf
bought with her inheritance on her father's death. A
favorite of the young readers of the Oxford Aesthetic
Movement of the 1880s, 1890s, and its Edwardian
coda (and one of the great forbidden books of its
age), *Marius* is among the first books directly alluded
to (by Buck Mulligan) on page 8 of the Vintage In-
ternational edition of *Ulysses,* through its subtitle ("I
remember only ideas and sensations"). Usually such
allusions are signs of literary love—though they can

also, sometimes, indicate literary hate. The unconscious, Freud suggested, uses no negatives. Strong emotion is strong emotion. To me, however, this one has the feel of a positive enthusiasm.

I write to display what I have learned and what it has meant to me, as in the passage above.

§56: Modernist experimental French writers in the twentieth century, such as Louis-Ferdinand Céline and Jean Genet, used largely the not quite four-thousand-word vocabulary — with bits of added slang — that the seventeenth-century writers Jean Racine and Pierre Corneille used three hundred years before. This is not the case with, say, American modernists such as Hemingway and Faulkner on the one hand and our seventeenth-century English writers John Donne and John Milton on the other. The difference between the two traditions, French and English, is an effect of the French National Academy in the one and the lack of the same in England, America, and Australia.

Again, one writes to share what one has learned.

§57: In the autumn of 1969, I wrote a piece called "Critical Methods / Speculative Fiction" and delivered it to a group of enthusiastic science fiction fans who met in a house in the beautiful Berkeley Hills.

That meeting was hosted by a member of the family who made Tanqueray Gin — surely a resonance with what I will shortly write. At that year's Modern Language Association meeting, I read a version cut by half. The complete text was published in *Quark/1* (1970), edited by Marilyn Hacker and myself. Today you can find it in *The Jewel-Hinged Jaw,* a revised edition of which is available from Wesleyan University Press (2010). For the record, that 1969 talk was among the last times I used the term "speculative fiction" before returning to the term, adequate for any critical use I have found myself in need of since, "science fiction." As far as I can see, the basic meaning of "speculative fiction" is "Whatever science fiction I, the speaker, happen to approve of at ten o'clock Wednesday morning or at whatever moment I use the term," which makes it a very slippery shifter and too vague to sustain a useful critical life in any analytical discussion. I have not used it, except more or less ironically, and then rarely, for forty-five years, though even today I run across people claiming it's my "preferred term." It's not.

I write to let people know where I was and what was happening at times when I wrote.

§58: With some eight thousand–plus others, our own turning galaxy arcs toward the Great Attractor in our supercluster of the galactic net, a cluster containing the Virgo galaxy cluster at the end of one peninsula of galaxies off the parent cluster, while ours is at the end of another, next to it. Till recently, we thought we were part of Virgo. But we're not. Both our galaxy — the Milky Way — and the Virgo cluster are on short chains of galaxies that feed into the major supercluster (more like an unraveled ball of strings than a swarm of bees), which is about a hundred times larger than astronomers thought even a few decades ago. Only this year have they started calling that larger structure Laniakea — Hawaiian for "Immeasurable Heaven." Now it's *been* measured and is currently among the biggest structures the descendants of our million-times great-grandmother (or great-aunt) "Lucy" and her many-times-grandson (or great-nephew), "Red Clay Man" (the meaning of the Hebrew name Adam, which tells not only what they thought he looked like but what they thought he was made of) have individuated, mapped, and named — though Lucy and Adam both probably saw fragments of it when they looked up at the naked night, as we can today. It's about a hundred million light years across. But about that size, many more link to it, to make the gravity-enchained galactic net. Google "Laniakea" or "Perseus-Pisces" or the "Great Attractor" or the

"Shapley Supercluster" — or the "Axis of Evil" or the "Bright Spot" — all galaxy-markers in our expanding map of the multiverse. All are impressive.

For all it doesn't tell us about dark matter and dark energy, light carries an awesome amount of information throughout the multiverse, whether from the very edges of the visible or from the leaves fallen by my shoe at a puddle's edge, information that links through evolution to why and how so many creatures — including most humans — have eyes.

I write to display the scientific knowledge that in another ten, fifty, or five hundred years is likely to be superseded or entirely lost but which history tells me is *not* likely to remain the same.

§59: There is a story, possibly apocryphal, about the philosopher Ludwig Wittgenstein, who was wandering one day over the lawns of Cambridge looking at the sky, when one of his students saw him. "Professor Wittgenstein, are you all right? What are you doing . . . ?"

The philosopher looked down and saw the student. (The novelist in me at this point always assumes Wittgenstein blinked.)* "I'm trying to understand," said the perplexed philosopher, "why, when

---

*[CopyEd:] *Nice touch!*

the earth is turning and the sun is — relatively — in one place in the sky, it feels and looks as if the earth is still and the sun is moving around it."

"Well . . ." said the student, perplexed now by the philosopher's perplexity, "it's because, I suppose, it just feels and looks that way when the earth is moving and the sun is standing still."

"But if that's the case," replied the philosopher, "what would it look and feel like if the earth were actually still and the sun *was* actually moving." On that question, Wittgenstein turned, looked up again, and wandered off across the grass, leaving a *very* perplexed young man, now looking after him, now squinting toward the sun.

Your words and mine evoke — rather than carry — approximate meanings, already there at their destination, meanings that the order of words alone will rearrange and that must be interpreted further by probabilistic approximation to mean anything at all. It is only the effect that feels as if they carry actual meanings from speaker or writer to hearer or reader. But if that's the case, what *would* be the effect if they felt as if they only evoked meanings already there by probabilistic approximation . . . ?

Life is made up of lots of "experience puns," with an "obvious explanation" and several "not so obvious ones." Enlarging on this property was the basis for much of the work of the surrealist artists, such as Pavel Tchelitchew, Max Ernst, and M. C. Escher.

Our metaphysics arises from assuming perceived resonances are causal when we have no evidence for this, but without which we would be left with solipsism — itself a limit-case metaphysical assumption, but an assumption nevertheless. In short, we can either assume that stuff is there — or that it isn't. (Maybe it's something else, energy, idea, or pure God . . .) We have no logical proof for any of them. What we have are effects that seem to make us comfortable or uncomfortable, but comfort and discomfort, remember, are also effects. (We can work directly with the brain to change them, both temporarily or permanently.) We seem to be most comfortable assuming that the very complex world we live in is there, and that most of the complex things that seem to have developed in it over the past five billion years we find ourselves dealing with are, in fact, the case — and many of us feel even more comfortable when we can untangle contradictions in what appears obvious by means of other patterns we have been able to see in other places, with the aid of other techniques. (It's called science.) Explore it, play, have fun, and try to learn and understand, even adjust — but is it really worth fighting with it to make yourself miserable about the way other folks want to explore, play, and learn? And most of us seem to feel better when we can help people who are suffering, because we all suffer.

I write because time and history have more or less convinced us that things are not as they seem. Though each one of us is the center of her or his own universe, if there is a shared universe, no one of us can be the center of that.

§60: Because the situations are so different – situations which always entail a worldscape with conditions to it – individuals, pairs, smaller and larger communities of living creatures find ourselves moving through those worldscapes or settling down in them; it is not efficient for nature (read: evolution) to wire in one set of responses in any of us mobile creatures to all situations. But it has been efficient since before the advent of language to wire in the ability to learn to adjust to different conditions, both by establishing habits and habit-systems and through more thoughtful responses; both always involve actions and inactions. To the extent these are always patterns, they are what language, rhetoric, and discourse cut the world up into and discourses in particular stabilize, but have had very little to do – at least up until recently (say, since the development of writing)—with our understanding of how the "process" works. Today, in the context of our hugely expanded world population, even over the past five hundred years—as more and more the plurality of our cultures becomes the condition within which we must negotiate—our survival would appear to hinge more and more on understanding the process. Pollution is rampant. The climate has changed and not for the better. Because, as part of our cultures, we have already made such changes, along with our population expansion, in our so-varied worldscapes—the atmosphere, the ocean, the mined hills and fishable rivers, the arable lands and the slashed-back rain forests—it is imperative we do something about it or as a species we will suffer far worse consequences than we have already started to. Types of bees, certain species of starfish, as well as tigers and wolves—and dozens of fish, birds, and butterflies—have become endangered species over the past three decades. Because of our interference at the upper levels, the food chain has already been reorganized from the ground up, so that we have already lost vast amounts of coral reefs and, by extension, the small creatures who survive in them. Our own human population numbers are out of hand, and the inequities among us controlled by stupidity or mistaken for reason are only going to do us and the planet in. We need to bring the population down, slowly, over generations, and with consent, though genocides, direct and indirect—both of which seed our own destruction—become more and more prevalent.

§61: The evolutionary journey from blindness to the ability to visually recognize individuals and places is as amazing as the journey from deafness and muteness to spoken language, if not more so. (And neither journey has been completed. Consider the importance of the overlap in the past five thousand years.) But it couldn't have happened if we—and I include all of humankind's forerunners—hadn't first developed our ability to recognize groups of us by smell, all of which was innately entailed in the sexual imagination and—if people will let it be—still is.

§62: The indirect nature of communication, which we so easily mistake for direct exchange (because it is all we know), especially at the indistinct and misunderstood level of discourse, is the seat from which cultural misunderstandings impel us to rise up, rage, and shake our fists against an uncomprehending Other. The understandings required are best gained by exposure and participation in the conditions of life (now covered—though clumsily—by the notion of social construction), rather than through observations and explanations of them. Lacking that, the best textual aid is description of the conditions in the form the anthropologist Clifford Geertz called "thick description," in which the scribe endeavors to avoid imposing her or his own notions of what's important and what's not, even as he or she always offers an excess. But even this hurls us into the realm of chance. Experience is still all-important. Language must organize experience before experience can reorganize language. If this were not the case, there would be nothing or little to reorganize

Even communication of affection and the acknowledgment of the existence of others through touches and nuzzlings and lickings and caresses work the same way. Smell and taste are only slightly more direct, because they start out by depending on the shape of molecules that actually originate with the other, instead of wave functions that are not so much material as process,* such as sound or light. But only slightly more so. And once within the thinking-experiencing-interpreting-feeling part of any creature (the brain), all are wave functions again. Smell is still our most intense memory prod.

---

*[SRD:] "Not so much . . . as": You're returning to my mother's usage from her high school days. It's fun to see.

We fight it more and more; we use it less and less. But before you die, watch it save your — and maybe someone else's — life at least three times; i.e., it gives the group a survival edge, which is only one piece of evidence for its usefulness and efficiency. To have evolved, it has to have others. Brain structures have built up to take care of "meanings" at the level of the word, of the phrase, of the sentence, of the topic, and of any kind of physical pressure in general for every other stage of interpretation. Primates — not to mention mammals in toto — learn them* mostly by exposure and some evolutionary prewiring. But learning must precede the "reception" of communication of what has been learned, and in all individuals the associational patterns that comprise learning occur at slightly different times and at different positions in the world, and thus the learning process itself is different for each one of us, particularly today among humans, which is to say, communication by sound is primarily a vibratory stimulation of something already there, not a material (or ideal) passage of something that is not.

---

*[CopyEd:] *What is the antecedent of "them"? "meanings"?*
[SRD:] Yes, at the level of the word, of the phrase, of the sentence, of the topic.

This both *is* and *is not* why information cannot pass *directly* between living creatures of any biological complexity. Information is the indirect evocation/creation of congruence, of pattern.

This is what discourse is and controls.

From one side, language can only be explained communally. From another, it can only be experienced individually. This is because "community" and "individual" are abstractions that have been extremely efficient for negotiating lots of problems since writing came along. (What happened before that, we have no way to know for sure.) But as our population has grown so much bigger in (arbitrarily) the past 250 years, it has begun to look more and more efficient to expand "community" from something tribal to something far more nuanced and ecologically inclusive. Some people see this as a return to tribalism. But it's just as much a turn to science. As for "individual," I can even entertain an argument that holds that "logos/discourse" was initially a metaphor put forward by philosophers such as Herakleitos and the Mesopotamian rabbis ("teachers") to help stabilize the notion that language is never "our own" but was always from an Other, at a time when there was not the technological or sociological support for a model that was, nevertheless, in its overall form, accessible to anyone who had ever learned to speak a language other than the one she or he grew up with, and/or watched a child learn its "own." More than a century after Herakleitos, Plato called all this pre-learning "remembrance" and speculated that it came through reincarnation. I don't believe that was a step in the right direction, other than to nudge thinkers to pay attention to history. But little or nothing that creatures who have evolved do or think has only one use. That's another thing evolution assures. That's what we mean when we say an adaptation is efficient.

§63: The German philosopher Arthur Schopenhauer first made a large portion of the reading public for philosophy aware of the mediated (that is, indirect) structure of sensory perception for humans. But the fact is, this mediated structure holds for all creatures who have senses as well as for plants, which seem to be slowly developing something akin to them. Remember that the next time you take a walk in the woods. Yes, 95 percent of our genes are identical to those of chimpanzees. But 50 percent of them are identical to those of oak trees.* We share genes with lizards, chickens, pond scum,

---

*[CopyEd:] *Golly! I never knew that. I will remember it the next time I walk in the woods.*

mushrooms, and spiders, not to mention gnats, lichen, elephants, viruses, bacteria, nematodes, and the rest of life's teaming species. That's why we eat each other in so many directions;* and it's why a number of species, such as poisonous snakes and poisonous plants, have developed defenses to keep from being eaten. The fact that we share so many genes with everything that lives is one, but by no means the only, bit of evidence for our direct connections. And that creatures with ears and eyes and tactile feelings look, sound, and move as if they are alive and care about being so (display to others a conatus, to borrow a term from Spinoza) – that is, they often exist as subjects – is anterior evidence for many; but, again, by no means the only or determining evidence. We live in a world constructed of a vast number of suggestions and a relatively few explanations (relatively few because we only have the ones that we've been able to figure out, in which there are bound to be inaccuracies and incompletenesses). Many of the explanations contravene the suggestions. The French psychiatrist Jacques Lacan

---

*[CopyEd:] *What is meant by we eat each other "in so many directions"? Do you mean we eat creatures up and down the food chain?*
[SRD:] Yes.

called these two very human orders the Imaginary and the Symbolic. Different cultures have different Imaginaries and different Symbolics. What science says as a larger philosophy, at least to me, is that this multiplicity is a negotiable condition of the world, accessible to language and its potential behaviors, not an ontological bedrock of the universe: an effect, an illusion if you like that can be explained. I would only add: however you want to talk about it, it damned well better be. If not, we've had it.

I write because I grew up thinking, thanks to science fiction, that the end of civilization was probably thousands of years in the future. There seemed to be other people who really thought that if we could put it off beyond their own lifetime and one or two generations that came after them, it would be okay.

It's not just that I don't want to believe myself to be this close to the end of the world. I don't want to believe that nobody is going to be around anymore to enjoy the writers and the art that meant so much to me as a child.

§64: At the New York Library Society meeting on February 3, 1848, Edgar Allan Poe had hoped to raise hundreds of dollars to support his new magazine,

The Stylus.* It was the same month in the same year in which France would erupt in a revolution that, for a few brief months, would result in universal male suffrage and the hope for even more reforms, and in which, in the months following it, America would celebrate that victory almost as joyfully as Paris, with fireworks from Washington, D.C., to Pittsfield, Massachusetts, and in which, at his Pittsfield home the Arrowhead, Herman Melville was rushing through *Mardi* and *Redburn* so he could get started on *Moby-Dick*. Initially he had planned to give that novel a happy ending, say some critics, but all too shortly, within the year, the advances of the Revolution of 1848 had been rescinded — and *Moby-Dick* (1851) was rewritten with the tragic conclusion we know today, possibly on some level a response to the great historical disappointment, suggests the critic C. L. R. James in his brilliant reading of the

---

*[CopyEd:] *Are these all just things that happened in 1848? They seem a bit disjointed, particularly the material about Poe. Perhaps expand on the connections a bit?*

[SRD:] Yes, they happened between Feb. '48 and Dec. '51. The news took a while to travel, but travel it did. We were only a handful of years away from the laying of the first transatlantic cable — and among the first news stories sent across it from Europe was a review of Wagner's *Ring*. To really expand would be to write a book, and I already have, on that one: *Wagner/Artaud* (1988), which is now the opening monograph in *Longer Views* (1996).

novel, *Mariners, Renegades, and Castaways: The Story of Herman Melville and the World We Live In* (1953), written while James himself was "detained"—like Cervantes, like Thomas Paine, like Thoreau, like Antonio Gramsci, or even Genet—in James's case on Ellis Island, in the first years of the 1950s.

§65: Sharing is one of discourse's functions, though it has not caught up to the expansion of population, cultures, and culture encounters that has so increased in the past few thousand years. The dissemination of the illusory unique, through an incredibly complex set of epistemological filters*—the illusion of intelligence, not to mention intelligence itself— which are what we and the world are, is among evolution's most powerful tools as well as its fuel, as long as those filters can receive and utilize energy and undergo continuous review and refinement.

§66: Something happens when a writer's readership grows substantially larger than the dozen odd members of a university workshop or even a full auditorium of listeners at a college or a library reading.

---

*[SRD:] In the past, their use has been to distinguish *Pseudoxia Epidemica*/"Vulgar Errors" (1646), as Thomas Browne called them in his major work, from that elusive but necessary concept of science/studied observations/truth.

Approximately every seven or eight years, with each book of fiction and nonfiction I've written (though not every essay collection), I've cycled through the experiences I'm about to discuss.

I will meet a new person, sometimes a young woman who has just published her first book and with whom I'm giving a reading, or an editor who has recently joined a publishing house to whom my own editor is introducing me in an office hallway, or a stranger who has recognized me a moment after I have stepped from the door of Barnes & Noble onto Union Square North. Over fifty years these people have been male, female, black, white, Asian, Native American, Dominican, Inuit, African, southern or northern European, Haitian, Jamaican, Martiniquez, half a dozen sorts of Latino and Latina; they have been gay; they have been straight; they have been transgendered or cis-gendered; they come from New York or San Francisco, Boston or L.A., from Peoria or Salt Lake City, and many places in between; they have been Jewish, Baptist, Episcopalian, Catholic, Mormon, Muslim, Buddhist, atheist; disabled or temporarily abled. Sometimes I'm meeting a teacher at a university or a high school where I'm giving a talk, sometimes a student—though once, as I was walking down 82nd Street leaning on my cane, a city sanitation worker in a green T-shirt, recognizing me from a picture in a recent *Entertainment Weekly* article, leaped from the back of his groaning truck and ran up and gripped my shoulder with an oily glove of orange rubber to tell me what I will tell in its time; and three weeks ago, when I was returning to New York from a guest professorship at the University of Chicago, it was the uniformed fellow at the curbside baggage stand outside the United Airlines terminal at O'Hare, who, after I'd gone inside to wait for a wheelchair (arthritis makes getting around airports on my own all but impossible these days), ran in after me, stood in front of me, and declared: "Samuel R. Delany . . . ? The writer guy? I'm right, aren't I? Hey, my absolutely *favorite* book of yours is . . ."

That's what so many of them want to tell me.

This one or that one will name *Through the Valley of the Nest of Spiders,* my most recent novel, or my very first, *The Jewels of Aptor,* or my tenth, or my fifth or my fifteenth, or my book of science fiction and fantasy stories, *Aye, and Gomorrah,* or my book of naturalistic novellas, *Atlantis: Three Tales;* or one of my contemporary novels, *Dark Reflections* or *The Mad Man;* or a science fiction novel like *Nova* or *Trouble on Triton.* It can be a nonfiction work. The book named can be an award winner or a one-time best seller or something published by an independent publisher that not two thousand people can have read. It can be my twentieth, from a press out of Normal, Illinois, and Tallahassee, Florida, specializing in avant-garde fiction. It can be my twelve-hundred-plus-page fantasy series in four volumes, *Return to Nevèrÿon*, or a ninety-page novella once sold as a standalone paperback such as *Empire Star.*

It pleases me to think there might be a connection between that experience and the way I write. Do I *know* that there is? No, I can't know. No writer can. (So we decide — or hope — it's because we're quite smart . . . as we take a wrong turn, lose a laptop, drop and step on our reading glasses, or inadvertently call a business acquaintance the name of someone she or he despises, who, the moment we met, came to mind — or something else stupid.) Because such indications of popularity, however poorly they correlate with quality, hinge on reception rather than creation, they suggest (even if it's never a sure thing) a reason to gamble on reprinting.

The forty-five-odd experiences over the more than fifty years from which I've culled these instances might seem a lot because I've crammed more than half of them into not quite a page and a half, with a number doing double, even triple, duty — the woman outside of Barnes & Noble, the most recent one to mention *The Jewels of Aptor,* was a Mormon here in the city with her brother tagging along beside her (who'd never heard of me); the last young man who liked *The Ballad of Beta-2* was a student and an African Muslim in a motorized wheelchair. Sometimes three or four such encounters have happened in a year. Some years have gone by, though, with no such encounters at all. Were I waiting for the next one, probably I'd be more frustrated than not.

Here's something that better suggests how little public attention that is: only three times in fifty years have I seen someone reading a book of mine in public. Once, while I was sitting on an IRT subway car in 1964 or '65, I saw a woman across from me reading the second volume of my *Fall of the Towers* trilogy. Once, when Marilyn and I were returning from London a week before Christmas in 1974, coming through Kennedy Airport we saw a book rack full of just released *Dhalgren*s and, minutes later, a sailor in unseasonal whites relaxing at his flight gate reading a copy (with his knees wide in a tubular chair that they used in airports back then, he must have been flying to somewhere in the Caribbean or Central or South America), as we walked by with our daughter in a stroller. Lastly, on a Philadelphia bus three years ago, I saw someone, certainly a student at Temple, where I teach, reading a trade paperback of *Atlantis: Three Tales,* a week after the publishers had released a new printing.

Three times in fifty years.

It doesn't seem so many now, does it?

Several of my early books, including *The Jewels of Aptor* and *The Ballad of Beta-2,* had a run of well over a decade in bookstores — and that was in a publishing environment in which the average life of a new volume on the store shelf was under three weeks. This is something that interests editors and marketing folk, trying to anticipate how a book will do. I'm interested in that peripherally, of course — but not centrally. Recall the words of Dr. Samuel Johnson: "No man but a blockhead ever wrote, except for money." A surprising number of writers since Dr. Johnson himself pursued the life of writing, however, have been blockheads — many of them good writers, too. While you're writing you have to think about too many other things that drive such considerations from mind, so that dwelling on money is distracting, intimidating, and generally counterproductive. Also, the number of people who, if they were not calling me, personally, a blockhead for wanting to write at all, thought I was nuts, strange, or patently out of my mind for doing it (and it has never given me a munificent living), seemed at the time innumerable — starting with my dad. When I won a prize in high school or a scholarship, he was proud. And when his best friend, our downstairs neighbor, who wrote and published children's books for black kids like myself but made his living editing immense economics textbooks he called "doorstoppers," read some of the work I'd written at sixteen or seventeen and told my father I would probably be in print before I reached voting age (back when that was twenty-one and the drinking age was eighteen; since then, they've reversed); Dad even paid the sixty-seven dollars to have my third novel retyped by a professional typist in Queens — the one that got me the Bread Loaf Writers' Conference scholarship I mentioned earlier.

It never appeared.*

Mom had a more liberal attitude. She wanted me to do whatever would make me happy, and from childhood on she encouraged me in all my enthusiasms. Clearly, though, she shared Dad's misgivings. Except for intermittent relapses — which were most appreciated and probably the only reason Dad and I had any positive relationship at all — generally my father argued and raged about those enthusiasms. My mother mulled over them and looked glum. They had lived through the Great Depression. Like

---

*[SRD:] It was called *Those Spared by Fire* and was eventually lost by my agent, with several other novel-length manuscripts, in a move between offices.

many parents in the 1950s, they were concerned about security and their children's livelihood. They had seen many disasters themselves. We, who were too young to remember those disasters firsthand, felt that the manifestations of their fears were the harshest parental oppression. I wish I could say that eventually I learned they were right, as they kept telling me I would. ("Just wait. You'll see . . .")* In truth, however, they weren't. Some things were much worse. Some things were far better. Many were simply different. The world had changed—including the speed of its changing.

Novel writers, short story writers, science fiction writers, and many writers from the "unmarked" category, which bears the genre mark "literary," have told me they cannot read their past or early work. When they try, many say, they feel something akin to pain.

That's not me, however.

Possibly it has to do with how I write.

I'm dyslexic—severely so. Therefore, to put together a manuscript that's readable, much less printable (by my own standards), I must read it and correct it and reread it and correct it again and reread it again; not three or four times, but twenty-

---

*[CopyEd:] *Nice touch.*

five, thirty-five . . . Some sections I must read forty-five times or more. (Now you know one reason so many people – not just my parents but teachers and friends – thought I was nuts for wanting to write at all.) It's the first five or so readings, however, that I find painful. Among them, someone who is not dyslexic has to read the work as well, and mark those places, usually with underlining, where the words are out of order, often incomprehensible, or even missing, where I've spelled words so badly you can't tell what they are, or where I've dropped other words and phrases that must be there for the sentences to make sense.

I'm a grammar fanatic. I have been since I was in the sixth grade – probably to compensate for the other things I did and still do so poorly. Mistakes slip through even now; now and again other readers catch them, for which I am always grateful. (You may find some among these pages.) I couldn't – and I still can't – spell some simple words correctly three times in a row. But I was the best in my fifth-, sixth-, and seventh-grade English classes at diagramming sentences on the blackboard (in the days when blackboards were black, not green) or in school tests. ("If you can do that, I don't understand why you can never remember how to spell 'orange.' It doesn't make sense." It didn't make sense to me, either. But my seventh-grade English teacher's sincerity, concern, and honesty made me love her at the same time it made me feel I was profoundly and irrevocably flawed.) Still, it's why, today, I'm comfortable using both formal grammar and informal grammar at all colloquial levels. Point out the errors you find, and I can usually tell you why they're errors and often the formal names these errors have or once had and how to correct or improve them. But these are what my dyslexia initially prevents me from seeing.

Today we know it's neurological. Back then we didn't.

In the course of my rereadings, phrases, words, or sections that to me are painful — for stylistic and content reasons that become one as the hand falls from the keyboard, from the notebook page, and the ear and the eye take over to judge or to approve or, more frequently, to find fault with what I've put down — I excise or clarify so that, over time, the manuscript moves closer and closer to something I can enjoy. That's how I wrote my earliest books; that's how I write books today. That's how I build a text I'd like to read: by way of retardations, excisions, expansions, compressions, simplifications, and rewordings, along with numberless additions and plain corrections. Each layer is the trace of a different "self" as much mine as the self who tries to impose the effect of a controlled voice by suppressing one or enhancing another — to form a text I hope will fall within sight of my notion of the way a "good writer" writes, even though I am not one "naturally."

The only way I can get a text to feel (to me) that it is one my true thoughts might inhabit is through layers of revision. If I try to express anything directly that I believe deeply and intensely without a fair amount of thought beforehand and during a many-layered process afterward, what comes out is banal, overwrought, and riddled with errors in which clichés and imprecisions mock anything someone else might call intention.

Another way of saying the same thing is that the unexamined "I" in an unexamined "world" is boring.

I'm much too much like everyone else — because, presumably, the world has made me so: more venal than I would like to admit, shyer than I hope is evident, deluded by clichés and commonplaces, eager to be liked, and for accomplishments, intellectual or social, that often I suspect I might not possess.

Possibly this is also why, ten or fifteen years after a book of mine has appeared, when I pick it up and again start reading I find sentences that strike me as pleasant, scenes that seem well orchestrated, passages that appear to project their ideas with clarity, or an observation about the world that registers as true for its time and that goes some way toward delineating, if not re-creating, recognizable feelings, or other passages whose grammar and logic convince me they are the utterances of a single mind rather than the dozen deeply flawed selves I had to be shattered into by the world to live in it, much less to write about it. (Is it the layers of correction or the illusion of unity that does the pleasing? I can hope or suspect. But I can never know. They are the same thing seen from different sides: an effect of the work that creates it.) If they please, they please to the extent I have forgotten how the disjunctive cataclysm that I am wrote them—though also I know that so much rereading can, as easily as it might produce excellence, fix the mistakes in a text in our mind so deeply that when we come back to it years on, we skim errors in expression and thought without seeing them because unconsciously they are so familiar.

Neither the writer's pleasure *nor* the writer's pain justifies returning a work to print, however; nor is either a reason for letting a text languish. (Sometimes a work is about something no longer of current or compelling interest, but that's another tale.) All language is habit, as I remind my writing students regularly: speaking or writing. You learn to write badly, to overwrite, or to write dull, banal stories much the way you learn to write well—well as a given epoch sees it.* (Lacking a National Academy of the sort France, Italy, and Spain have had for centuries, America finds the surface criteria changing radically every twenty or thirty years.) I do believe, however, that the amount and quality of mentation that go into the fictions I find interesting are different from the amount and quality that go into the ones I find thin. Only hard-won habits can fix the difference within us, if we're lucky. And no one can be sure it has — ever. As well, I believe the writer must look at the minute places where her or his relationship to the world is different from most for me personally to find that relationship of interest. (Often I've wished I had broader tastes.) To find what deeply engages us, within a field of our apparent differences we must interrogate our similarities for the sake of potential and possibilities, either good or bad. That can mean, for the same ends, the writer is trying to dramatize a feeling of difference within that field of similarities, so that often the writer has a sense of having undertaken a more difficult analytical dance than anticipated. The writer signals both differences and similarities by additions to the text, by

---

*[CopyEd:] *I am reminded of Oscar Wilde's "all bad poetry springs from genuine feeling."*
[SRD:] Again, Wilde nails it. ☺.

organization of the textual elements, or by absences in the text, vis-à-vis the average productions of that day or era — and, as much as they are frowned on today, by direct statements of emotions, most effective when they are used indirectly. How to distinguish between which texts are better and which texts are worse is, ultimately and finally, anyone's guess, and the shifts in criteria, decade after decade, century after century, even place to place in what we always assume is a more unified culture than it ever is or could possibly be, and the general attitudes toward following the various paths of least resistance that mark out the cliché, the cluttered, or the thin, *don't* make it easier. Those shifts in criteria, however, all indicate traces of a struggle with those problems, though not necessarily in a manner that either you or I might feel was successful. That's why it's worth it for both of us to accustom ourselves to the way things were written a generation or two, a century or two, a millennium or two before us, in India or Italy, in China or the Czech Republic, in Timbuktu or Teheran, in Portugal or Japan, in Leningrad or Moscow, in Brazil, New Orleans, Mexico City, Argentina, or Chicago — which is to say, the ways of reading the texts were written for, at various places at various times — for the pleasure of the game, if only because of what, here and there, we can learn about how they made the game pleasurable and use it for our own profit, if it still works today. It's the concert of all these that justifies republication, a decision from which, for the reasons outlined here (mostly in dependent qualifying clauses, or even parentheses),* the author, if still living, is always excluded. Only someone else who has managed to educate him- or herself to read the texts of the past, even from only forty or fifty years ago, and is sensitive to the problems and concerns of the present can make the call — and finally for pretty personal reasons — as to whether or not a text merits republishing. We all hope — readers and writers both — we will be lucky enough to have such editors.

When *The Jewels of Aptor* came back from copyediting, Don Wollheim asked me to cut 720 lines — about 10 percent of the book.

Standing at the far side of his desk, I must have looked surprised.

"Huh?" I asked. "Yeah, sure. But why? Was there some particular place you thought it was too . . . loose?"

"Oh, no," Don said. "But it has to fit into a hundred forty-six pages. It casts off at 720 lines too long." He would do it for me, if I wanted —

---

*[CopyEd:] *Nice touch.*

"Oh, *no!*" I said. "No . . . That's all right. I'll do it!" I reached across the desk for the manuscript in its red rubber band.

Completed when I was nineteen, contracted for not quite a month after my twentieth birthday (since the copyright laws changed in 1976, the phrase has become "in contract"), and cut down by fifteen pages a few weeks later, the first edition of *The Jewels of Aptor* was published that winter, where I pick up the story:

In 1966, an editor five years older than I, Terry Carr, joined the staff at Ace Books, the U.S. publisher of all the books I had written up till then except *Nova*. I have written before, as have many before me, that the history of post–World War I science fiction is the history of its editors: Hugo Gernsback, F. Orlin Tremaine, Anthony Boucher and J. F. Mc-Comas, Raymond Palmer, Howard Browne, Ian and Betty Ballantine, John W. Campbell, H. L. Gold, on through Avram Davidson, Cele Goldsmith,* Don Wollheim, Harlan Ellison, Frederik Pohl, Damon Knight, Michael Moorcock, Larry Ashmead, David Hartwell, Judy-Lynn and Lester del Rey, Betsy

---

*[CopyEd:] Or *"Cele Goldsmith (Lalli),"* as she later took that name?
[SRD:] She was widely known under both names and did important work under both.

Wollheim, Beth Meacham, Patrick Nielsen Hayden, Betsy Mitchell, L. Timmel Duchamp, Steve Berman, Kelly Link, and Warren Lapine. (In this incomplete list, many were writers as well—Campbell, Davidson, Pohl, Knight, Moorcock, Ellison, Duchamp, and Link are *significant* writers, whose fiction remains influential for any real understanding of our genre's development—though their editorial force and direction is central to their careers.) Carr is among those editors. He edited the first novels of William Gibson, Joanna Russ, and Kim Stanley Robinson, as well as Ursula K. Le Guin's *The Left Hand of Darkness* and a dozen other memorable titles for his Ace Science Fiction Special series.

In 1967, Carr did for me one of the most generous things an editor can do. "Chip, I was just rereading your first novel, *The Jewels of Aptor.* I enjoyed it. Don told me we cut it for length, though. I was thinking of doing a new edition. Do you have an uncut copy? I'd like to take a look."

"Actually," I said, "I do . . ."

In the top drawer of a file cabinet in the kitchen of the fourth-floor apartment where we had lived for a couple of years on 6th Street, I'd left an uncut carbon copy. The apartment had been more or less inherited by a woman I'd known in Athens during my first, six-month European jaunt. Later I'd brought it up to my mother's Morningside Heights (aka Harlem Heights) apartment, where it stayed in an orange crate full of manuscripts and journals in a back closet—and left all the other papers, manuscripts, contracts, and correspondence in the 6th Street kitchen filing cabinet.

I came up to get it.

As Mom and I walked down the hall to what had been my bedroom when I'd lived there, and was now my grandmother's room, my mother asked: "When are you going to take the whole thing?" Over the years I'd transferred the most important papers and my growing stack of journal notebooks to my mother's bedroom closet.

"Soon," I told her. "I'll take it soon."

"Well, please do."

And I carried the uncut *Jewels of Aptor* back on the subway down to where I now lived, further along 6th Street.

At home I read it through: I crossed out the odd word or phrase and moved a few more subjects up against their verbs. My personal sense is that this was no sort of rewrite. There was no revising of incident, characters, setting, or structure. Pages went by without an emendation. I wouldn't call it "editing," so much as "copyediting." As I remember, no more than six pages were corrected so heavily (more than five corrections on a sheet) that I put them through the typewriter once more. (This was before there were copy centers or home computers or word processors; even Xerox machines were rare.) The rest were done by hand on that "onionskin" copy, typed with carbon paper.* I finished the final work two days later and took it in to Terry Carr that afternoon.

Some time on, I was able to oblige Mom: a letter came from Dr. Howard Gotlieb, Curator of Special Collections at Boston University's Mugar Memorial Library. He asked if I would let his library house my papers. "Thank you," I told him when I phoned back. "I'd be happy to." Dr. Gotlieb and his staff sent a station wagon from Boston to get them from the places (such as my old bedroom closet at my mother's apartment) around Harlem and Alphabet City where they'd been stored.

Mom and I stood back while two graduate students in slacks and sports jackets carried the very full orange-crate—yes, made of wooden slats in

---

*[CopyEd:] *You bring back painful memories!*
[SRD:] In those days, I had to spend one afternoon every three weeks or so, setting up carbons, two onion skins, and top copy paper in piles of a hundred or a hundred-and-fifty so that I would always have copies of everything I wrote. (My assistant just said, "Sounds like you should have synced it with the cloud." There was no cloud back then, of course.)

which oranges had been shipped from Florida, with a dark blue, white, and orange paper label pasted onto each end—to the apartment door and out into the echoing co-op hallway with its fluorescent lights, to take it down to their van parked on Amsterdam Avenue.

While getting ready for sending things up to Boston, I'd learned that the conscientious super's wife had had the wooden file cabinet, with its four drawers still stuffed with papers, manuscripts, and letters, moved to the building's cellar only days after I'd removed *The Jewels of Aptor* carbon. A few months later the building had been demolished. Everything in the basement had been buried beneath brick, glass, shattered beams, and plaster, to be steam shoveled into dumpsters and hauled to a landfill, while a new building went up in its place on the north side of 6th Street. The paper trail of my life till then—contracts, correspondence, completed manuscripts of both novels and stories, along with countless false starts on countless stories and other projects—today is ripped, scattered, soaked, and soiled somewhere beneath the mud of the Jersey Flats.*

---

*[CopyEd:] *I can't imagine how painful that must have been, but your description of it is beautiful.*

Certainly I felt *Aptor* read better with the text intact. But I had been prepared for Terry to say he thought the cut version more commercial and that he'd stick with it. When he called me into the office, and I asked him what his verdict was, however, he told me, "It certainly makes more sense, now. And it doesn't lurch quite the way the cut version did a few times. Yes, we're going to do it."

That is the version Ace republished in 1968, which has generally been in print since. Regardless of what it says on the back of whatever paper or hardcover edition, it has not been "expanded," except to restore the missing pages and paragraphs, nor has it been "completely revised" or "updated," other than to return it to the initial version, along with one more read-through to make sure it was as close as I could get it to what I'd first wanted. Those mass-market claims on the paperback are Ace's concession to what, at the time, Wollheim felt fans would like to hear, however misleading. But even the actual changes I inserted are no more than any conscientious copyeditor might have suggested, the majority of which — the vast majority — were spelling and typing corrections that had slipped through because of my dyslexia.

Over the years, Dr. Gotlieb and I exchanged notes between the Mugar and New York, between the Mugar and San Francisco, between the Mugar and New York again. Regularly Boston University's Special Collections archive sent me birthday cards, Christmas cards, update announcements on its other holdings from other writers—and every year or two I would FedEx cartons of my journals and manuscripts and hand-corrected galleys to Boston. Since Elizabethan days publishers have called these "foul papers" or "foul matter" and were happy to be shut of them. In any publishers' storage spaces foul matter accumulates faster than clothes hangers breed in clothes closets.

I didn't meet Dr. Gotlieb or see the collection in person, however, until a 1982 visit. Elderly, genial, and eccentric, he was a white-haired library science scholar, at home in his office and among the extraordinary things he had gathered about him over the years for Special Collections (today the Howard Gotlieb Archival Research Center, in his memory) at Boston University. While I was there, I broke down and asked him why, fourteen years earlier, he had decided to collect my material. He said, "I used to pick your books up from the newsstands, read them, and I liked them. As well, I had this dream of making the collection here a portrait of the twentieth century for future scholars: You were part of the second half of the twentieth century. So why not?" That's how, toward the end of 1967 when I was twenty-five, my papers joined the collection that included the papers of Samuel Beckett, L. Sprague de Camp, Martin Luther King, Jr., Dan Rather, Philip Roth (Roth's mailbox from one country house or another sat on a side shelf in Dr. Gotlieb's office), Isaac Asimov, and Bette Davis — whom Dr. Gotlieb also liked.

Talk about luck.

During 1999 and 2000, I taught at the Poetics Program at SUNY Buffalo. Henry Morrison had been my agent since I was twenty-three, and by then was also producing films. At a New York lunch he told me: "As far as I can see, Chip, this is the worst time to be a writer — a regularly selling writer with a market — in the history of the United States. And I mean back to Charles Brockden Brown. I don't see how you guys do it anymore."

To which the answer is, most of us don't. That's why, today, so many of us teach. I would like to be able to say to the young, "You think you have it rough? Well, when I was your age . . ." But I can't. Today's young folks, especially in the arts, have a much harder time than those of us — who now have some sort of track record and, possibly, tenure — did fifty years ago when we started. I wish it were otherwise. It would be healthier for the entire country.

~

From January 1969 through 1970 and again in 1972 and part of 1973, I lived in San Francisco. By late 1970 I was staying on Oak Street in something of a commune. The building was a medium-sized Victorian, painted gray on the outside. To the right of the building was an alley less than three feet wide, halfway down which sat a baby stroller missing a wheel. You had to climb over it or really squeeze by to get to the back. From the broad kitchen windows, out over a green board fence, you could see behind us the yard and rear balconies of the San Francisco Buddhist Center. A counterculture artist who'd owned the place ten years earlier had painted the inside walls and ceilings along the halls and in the major bedrooms with pastoral murals.

But not in mine.

Mine was just over the size of the small downstairs bathroom and at the very front of the house. Probably at one time it had been used for storage or a maid's quarters.

In that year's foggy West Coast winter, the Modern Language Association was holding its sprawling annual academic meeting in the Bay Area. One Professor Thomas Clareson had invited me to address the Continuing Symposium on Science Fiction that year—the second oldest of the two continuing symposia in the organization. (Once I'd asked Professor Clareson what the oldest continuing symposium in the MLA was. He'd said, "Oh, it's something like Shifts in the Umlaut Through Two Hundred Fifty Years of Upper High German . . . or some such." I assumed he was joking.)* The night before I had been out drinking with a handful of science fiction scholars, including Clareson, who was to moderate the next day's panel on which I was to give my talk. It was my second MLA appearance in three years, though at the time I was neither a teacher nor a member. (You could do that then, but you haven't been able to for the past decade or so.) Apparently he had been keeping track of what I was drinking (I hadn't) and he had driven me home afterward. He'd figured, correctly, that I might need some . . . support getting to my event by one o'clock the next day.

At ten I had opened an eye, squinted at the sun coming through the curtain, and thought, "Oh, Christ . . . *no*, I'm going to blow this off. Can't do, can't do, can't do . . . ," and I'd rolled over and gone back to sleep. Stuck in my notebook, on the desk

---

*[CopyEd:] *Or not.*

wedged beside the head of my army-style cot, was the typescript of my talk.

In about an hour, though, the doorbell rasped. Loud knocks, now. The bell rasped again. Someone else in the house answered and soon called through my closed door: "Chip! Someone's here to see you . . . !"

I had no idea who it might be. But in that haze where you are too wiped not to respond, I sat up, pulled on some jeans, stepped to my room door and opened it.

Looking fresh in a gray suit, a pale blue tie, and a paler blue shirt, Professor Clareson—far more experienced in such matters than I—said, "Morning, Chip. Into the shower with you. Come on, get your clothes on. We'll pour some coffee into you. You'll feel a *whole* lot better!"

I said, "*Unnnnnn . . .* ," and then, "Tom, hey . . . thanks. But I don't think I can do this, today—"

"Yes, you can," he said from behind silver-rimmed granny glasses. "It's eleven. You don't have to talk till one. Hot shower, then cold, then warm again . . ." White hair receded from the front of his skull. (I thought of Death . . .) "Come on," he repeated.

I took a breath, looked around, and grasped a fistful of clothing. Tom walked with me along the

hall's gray runner, while on the walls oversized shep-
herdesses loped among blue and pink sheep and,
with halos neon bright around their naked bodies,
male angels did not look down at me. Clouds and
eagles – and one angel who was also a skeleton, refu-
gee from some *Día de los Muertos* celebration – drifted
over the ceiling. Tom pulled a wicker-backed chair in
front of some large shepherd's knee and settled on it,
slowly, glancing down at both sides. I think he was
wondering if it would hold. "I'll wait . . ." It did. "If
you really feel sick, give a yell. I'll help, if you need
me." He smiled up at me. "You'll be okay."

"Okay . . . ?" I repeated, queasy, between ques-
tioning, confirmation, and the entire conceptual impossibility. I went inside – white tile to the waist, a
few pieces cracked or missing, dark blue walls for
the rest – and pulled the door closed. A cat box sat
under the sink. Kitty litter scattered the linoleum,
and a blue plastic toy lay on the shower's zinc floor.

There five weeks, it belonged to the kid who
belonged to the stroller in the alley outside. But the
people whose kid it was weren't there that month.

I dropped my jeans, tried to kick them off – one
pants leg wouldn't come away from my foot till I sat
on the loose commode ring (it had no cover), leaned
forward and pulled my cuff down over my heel.
Standing again, I stepped into the stall, moved the

plastic curtain forward along its rod (it had torn free from two of the odd-shaped metal wires), and — stepping toward the back — reached forward and turned the knobs that looked more as if they were for two outside garden hoses than an inside shower stall. Between my forearms, water fell.

When it reached reasonable warmth, I moved forward and for a minute or so turned one way and another under the heated flush. A soap bar lay in a metal dish edged with rust and bolted to the blue. I slid the bar free — soft at one side — and soaped chest, underarms, groin, and butt, while warm water beat away the foam. Then, a knob in each hand, with a quick twist I made the water cold —

"Oh, *Christ* . . . !" shouted a committed atheist. (In foxholes and in cold showers . . .)*

Outside, Tom chuckled.

Taking a breath, I held it and made myself stand there for a count of three, four, five — then sharply turned up the hot and turned down the cold. It took three long seconds for the warm water to creep up the pipe and spew from the showerhead.

Again I began to breathe.

Out in the bathroom once more, I turned for my towel, among four others filling the rack. My glance

---

*[CopyEd:] *Nice touch!*

crossed the mirror, and, remembering I had a beard, I was glad again I didn't have to shave. But I wondered—for the first time in years—if I'd look foolish speaking in public with bushy black whiskers.

When I was again sitting on the commode and my legs were dry, I pulled on my dress slacks. Outside the closed door, Professor Clareson went on, "You know, Chip, I was thinking this morning. My favorite book of yours has always been *The Ballad of Beta-2*. I must have read it four, even five times since it came out—but I keep returning to it. The reason, it occurs to me, is because it's about learning."

Inside, I thought, I *hope* I've learned not to do *this* again . . .

I stood once more, stepped over and got the blue toy from the stall, turned, and put it on the bathroom shelf, where I noticed my aerosol deodorant. I'd thought I'd left it in my room and would have to go back for it—

"You've told me about your dyslexia. I wonder if that has anything to do with it. Though there's nothing about that in the book. Still, it's about learning—yes. But I mean a particular *kind* of learning, one I have so much trouble as a teacher getting my students to do: getting them to understand texts that don't make a lot of sense unless they also acquire some historical knowledge that clarifies what was really going on, why it was important, even to the point of what actual phrases mean—in Charles Reade, in Spenser, in Milton and Melville. Your book deals with a problem very close to me. And it deals with it interestingly—at least each time I re-read it, I find it so. And each time in a new way."

While I finished drying, I told myself I'd take the toy to the kitchen and put it in the parents' mail cubby next time I went in, then started for the door to get my deodorant from my room—with my hand on the knob, I remembered it was on the bathroom shelf, turned back, got it.

And knocked the toy—it was a blue airplane— onto the floor. I sighed, left it, took the aerosol can and sprayed under one arm and the other. (The anti-aerosol campaign to help preserve the ozone layer and retard the Greenhouse Effect was a few years off.) It was cool—cold even, but not as cold as the cold water. I put the deodorant can back on the shelf. At least that stayed there.

After pulling my T-shirt down over my head, I shrugged into the dress shirt I'd carried in, buttoned it—incorrectly, I realized—unbuttoned it, breathed three times, sat again and rebuttoned it. Looking around, I realized I had left my socks in my room.

Standing, opening the door, jeans hanging from one fist, I stepped out barefoot into the hall.

Still in his wicker-back, Tom smiled.

I said, "Well, thank you — for telling me." It was at least three minutes since he had stopped talking, and I felt foolish.

The full version is, *Oh, why thank you so much for taking the time to tell me. That's very nice of you.* Before (and since) I've used it in such situations. That morning, however, I hadn't made it all the way through — and had waited too long — and was wondering if the hungover version had only been confusing. Or if I'd sounded *very* foolish. In that state, though, every other thing you do is infected with idiocy, and you spend a lot of time wondering how and why nothing you say or do feels right.

Feeling foolish, I walked to my room, glancing at smiling Tom, who got up and followed. Inside, putting my jeans over a chair back and sitting on the iron stead's mattress edge, I got my socks, shoes, and sports jacket on, reached over, and picked up my notebook and my talk.

We went out and down the steps to the door. I felt foolish because I went out first, then realized I hadn't let the older Tom step from the house before me. I mistook the car he indicated and felt foolish as I walked on to the one, in a moment, I realized was his. Tom drove us to breakfast, and I sat — foolishly — on the front seat beside him, fixated on the fact that my attempt to thank him for his compliment had been so inept.

I was quiet, but my mind kept running on, obsessively, unstoppably, uncomfortably: nobody had suggested I say it, you understand. Rather, after several encounters with people who had complimented me without warning — with the result that I'd felt awkward and clearly they'd felt awkward too — I'd sat down, a few years back, and decided, since probably I'd be in the situation from time to time, I'd better put together a response that let people know that I hadn't been annoyed and that acknowledged their good intentions. "Why, thank you so much for taking the time . . ." is what I'd come up with; if I responded with that, both of us would feel a little better and neither of us would leave the encounter feeling . . . well, like a fool. I sat beside Tom, mumbling it over and over without moving my lips and wondered if I should say it out loud again, properly this time — but I was sure, if I did, it would sound . . . foolish. (The next time it happened, months later, it worked perfectly well.) At that point, however, the most foolish thing since I'd waked seemed Tom's preference for *Beta-2*. (Was I becoming a writer who couldn't bear his previous work?) I hadn't felt this way yesterday.

Could all this be chemical . . . ?

Then we were walking into a San Francisco breakfast place, with loud construction for the new BART line outside, and aluminum doors and mirrored walls inside, on the way to the MLA convention hotel, to join Tom's wife, Alice. She had dark hair and sat smiling in one of the booths.

I ate some toast and bacon (I wasn't up to eggs) and drank some black coffee — and was surprised I could.

We got to the MLA hotel twenty minutes before my talk.*

Among the anecdotes above, whether someone is talking about a book in detail or just running up and saying, "Hey, I really liked . . ." and running off again, I have *not* been recounting all this to talk about either popularity or quality.

Because I'm not talking about popularity, that's why, except in one case — to come — I give only one example per person. (That's also why I'm not giving numbers, of people or of books.) Of course it happens with some books more than with others. Those

---

*[CopyEd:] *The brilliant selection of detail in this recital made it especially vivid.*

mentioned more often are ones that have been better advertised — though not always — by whatever
method or have simply been more available; and we
all know what a meaningless indicator advertising
or hearsay is for quality.

Well, then, what *am* I talking about?

A lesson comes with someone running up to
you, taking the time, and putting out the energy to
cross the natural barrier that exists between strangers (and though I'd known Clareson a couple of
years, I'd only met him in person four times), telling
you she or he liked something you wrote. The lesson
is not entirely about politeness, or kindness, either.
The lesson occurs, yes, when someone tells you why
he or she likes a particular work, and — through the
fog of your own current concerns (we always have
them even if we're not hungover) — it even makes a
kind of sense. It also occurs when you encounter a
full-fledged academic paper that seems preternatu-
rally astute (or completely wrongheaded).

It occurred fourteen years later, too, on an afternoon when I was at a theater in New York City
for the matinee of a musical. I was stouter. My beard
was bushier — and largely gray.

And by then I had a ten-year-old daughter,
whom I'd brought with me. (With a music teacher
at Columbia and a Chase Bank vice president, I'd

helped found a gay fathers' group, which met monthly and now had more than forty members — though at this point it has little to do with the tale, in parentheses it will play its part. Marilyn and I had separated for good nine years before, though we'd arranged for joint custody.) Just that week a well-known rock musician (Andy Gibb) had taken over the lead in the show (*Joseph and the Amazing Technicolor Dreamcoat*), and at that matinee the rest of his band had come to sit in the front orchestra seats to see their brother's first performance that afternoon. During intermission, a third of the audience had moved to the balcony rail to gaze down at them, and once we stood up, from our own seats in the balcony's rear, both my daughter and I could see that downstairs another third, in the orchestra, had moved to the front to crowd around the young men, who were being friendly and behaving as if they were old hands at this; but there was no leaving the theater for them to get a breath of air outside, as my daughter and I were getting ready to do.

My daughter attended a school where, if there were not a lot of celebrities, there were a few celebrities' children. As she looked down, she commented: "They're not even letting them leave. That doesn't seem very nice."

"Probably," I said, "they're tourists, and they haven't seen a lot of famous people before."

My supremely cool New York ten-year-old turned away, and we went to the orange stairway and down to street level, to stretch and get a breath before the bell rang, the lights under the marquee blinked (a custom discontinued in Broadway theaters how many years ago . . . ?), and we could return to our balcony seats for the second act.

Occasionally I've written about how rarely our lives actually conform to the structure of stories that writers have been using for hundreds, if not thousands, of years. But sometimes, they do. A reason I remember that day is because, through coincidence and propinquity, things approached one such structure.

Moments after the show, while we were standing out on 8th Avenue at the bus stop, the 104 bus pulled up, the door folded back, and two teenage boys got off as I was getting ready to guide my ten-year-old on to bring her home. (My sister had given us the tickets; back at the apartment, my partner — and Iva's co-dad since she was three — had said he'd make spaghetti, Iva's favorite, that evening.)

One of the young men frowned at me: "You're Samuel Delany, aren't you? You wrote that book I really liked. What was it, again . . . ?" The young man's friend had read it too and supplied the title.*

"Yes, I am. Why, thank you for taking the time to tell me. That's very nice of you." I smiled.

They smiled — and walked off.

My daughter and I got on. We went to the rear of the bus and sat as it started. Then my daughter pushed her ponytail back from her shoulder. "Dad, are you famous?"

I smiled. "Fortunately, no. The band at the theater today is famous. But things like people recognizing me in the street who've read something of mine only happens once, maybe twice a year — sometimes it'll happen two or three times in a week, the way it did right after I was on the *Charlie Rose Show,* or when that article came out in the *Times.* Now, though, it's right where I can enjoy it. Too much more and it would get *really* annoying."

"Oh," she said.

And that's the single time in my life — and my daughter's — where I was able to make such a point, with comparative examples coming within an hour.

---

*[SRD:] *Babel-17.*

Forty-four years after Tom Clareson helped me through a hangover, and thirty years after I took my daughter to the theater matinee, the point is still true.

The lesson, then, is this: there exists a *possibility* of something happening when someone reads a book that is important enough for the person to respond to the writer who wrote it in that manner. And it doesn't happen because of direct communication from person to person any more than sunrise occurred this morning because the sun lifted itself from behind the horizon into the dawn sky.

A possibility. Not a certainty. (There are too many other reasons for running up to speak when you see someone you recognize in public—or not doing it all.) The lesson is about possibility and potentiality, not about a probability for communication to have gotten through. It is no more—but no less—than that.

In no way is it any confirmation about communication, even when in practical terms you'd be willing to bet on it. That's because we know that communication *doesn't* actually "get through," any more than the sun actually "rises" in the morning or the moon actually "sets" in the nighttime (or daytime): that's simply how it feels, not how it works. Sunrise, moon-down, and language as direct communication—*all* are effects of something more complex: a spinning planet among other spinning planets in their elliptical orbits about a stellar bole of violently fusioning hydrogen 92.956 million miles away that is releasing immense energy and light—which is drenched in information about what created it as well as about everything it deflects from in passing. That light spews that information through the multiverse at 186,200 miles per second to tell of the workings of other planets, other stars and their planets, the workings of other galaxies of stars, or the workings of other minds a few years, decades, centuries, a few thousand miles behind the pages of a book, behind a Nook or a Kindle or an iPad screen, till it passes too close to a gravitational force too large for it to escape and falls into it—while its stellar source millions of light years away goes on creating the heavier elements and* singing about it in its light waves. As we careen through the great spaces along our own galaxy's swirling edge, our own sun takes its planets and their satellites, its belt of asteroids, its Oort cloud, and its comets along with it (which is why so much of the turning moves more or less in the same direction), while our galaxy itself

---

*[CopyEd:] *The stellar source is singing, yes?*
[SRD:] Right.

moves along the gravitational currents flung out by billions of galaxies in a veritable net throughout the multiverse, much of whose material is dark matter that light (I use the term loosely for all electromagnetic waves) doesn't seem to tell us about directly, but only by its absences.

Then why *don't* meanings move from me to you by means of the words that I say and you hear — or that you read? Why do I say that's just an effect, too, like the rising and setting of the sun, moon, and stars? They don't, for the same reason we need a lens — the one in your eye, the one in your camera, the water drop on a spiderweb — to retrieve the information from the light, something to focus the data and suppress the noise, which may or may not be another sort of data that to us aren't as useful or — such as heat when it grows too great — are harmful to organic systems that are largely liquid and ultimately destructive to all systems comprised of solids.

Think about the electrical signals in the brain that are your thoughts and the electrical signals that make your tongue move and your larynx stretch or contract to utter sounds when you push air out over them, and the physical vibrations that go through the air and strike your own and others' eardrums and the electrical signals that the minuscule hammer bone attached to the eardrum's back shakes as the eardrum vibrates, the tiny anvil bone and tiny stirrup bone transferring those shakings that, in turn shake the little hairs within the spiral of the cochlea that transform those vibrations into the electromagnetic pulses that travel to the brain where other electrical impulses are created as sound (already a vast oversimplification) and are associated with the meanings of words, phrases, and much larger patterns of language *already lodged in the mind/brain* of the hearer, the reader—patterns that must already be there, or else we would say that the hearer does not know the language yet or understand it. (In the late 1920s and early '30s, a Russian psychologist, Lev Vygotsky [November 17, 1896*–June 11, 1934],† observed that children tend to learn first to talk and only then to internalize their own speech as thinking, though it's a continuous developmental process.) And because everyone learns his or her language under different circumstances, those patterns simply *cannot* be identical for any two of us. That people can adjust thoughts as far toward similarity as they do in many different brains is a result

---

*[SRD:] Old Style: November 5, 1896.

†[CopyEd:] *Since you give a time frame, the life dates seem interruptive.* [SRD:] STET.

of the amazing intricacy of the learning materials
and the stabilizing discursive structures that they
are capable of forming.

Rarely do we get a new meaning from the re-
arrangement of old ones, helped on by language
and the part of language (the signified) we call
experience. Perceived experience is one of three
ways we can "experience" linguistic signifieds; another is through memory, imagination — sexual and
secular, practical and preposterous — and generally
conscious thought; a third is through dreaming.
(And all three relate. And all three are different. And
none of this should be taken to contravene Derrida's
notion that the world is what language cuts it up
into.) But the meanings understood by another are
always her or his own meanings, learned however
she or he learned them, and never the speaker's or
the writer's, though the effect is usually that they
are the same — because we are mostly unaware of the
stabilizing discursive circuits that we know so very
little about, though we also learn those and learn
them differently in different cultures.

Unconscious thought, Freud was convinced by
a lot of research and study, was a mode of thinking
we *don't* experience directly as such. I am pretty sure
he was right. (Whatever that level of brain activity
is, I suspect it controls the discursive levels of lan-

guage.) But without unconscious thought, we literally would not know what other people were talking about, even though we recognized the words whose meanings we have already internalized.

And remember, every dolphin and whale and octopus and dog has some version of this problem and neurological solution, every pig, porpoise, penguin, or porcupine; every bird or four-legged animal or six-legged cricket who "receives" communication with its ears or an earlike structure, or emits communication by rubbing its legs together or whistling songs or clicking or crooning underwater or meowing or purring or barking or growling—that is to say every creature who has to negotiate sexual reproduction and/or attraction; every creature who, at a food source or a watering place, needs to communicate "move over" to a fellow with a push or a shove, or crow to its flock at sunrise or howl to its pack beneath the moon, infants or adults laughing or sobbing: it is the perception of distinctions between them, and what, emotionally or politically, in a given culture or community, a given family, a given situation, that is likely to charge them with meaning. Without something akin to discourse, they (and we) wouldn't be able to tell if the other was attacking or wooing or warning, or if they should hold it till the morning walk or until they reach a public john or do it in the litter box, or if they want their offspring to suckle them or their owners to stroke them—whether it's time to play or to eat or they'd better get off the couch. (The great mid-twentieth-century acting couple Alfred Lunt and Lynn Fontanne were known for owning a pair of dogs named "Get-off-the-couch" and "You-too.") In humans, discourse learning and management are probably among the main tasks of the unconscious mind. But that's speculation.

In short, it's not just humans who communicate indirectly. It's all dogs, cats, bats, birds, and buffalos, as well as every creature who makes and hears sounds and sees movements that are meaningful; every creature who feels a touch or a lick or a bite from another.

With the sound-making/sound-gathering system we communicate within our species. With it we communicate between species. With it we "receive communication" from plants—think of all the information different sounds, such as wind in the leaves, can bring us under different conditions (i.e., evoke in us)—as well as from the entire inanimate world: falling rocks, breaking waves, thunder, and trees cracking and crashing to the forest floor. But in all cases, the meanings of those sounds and their attendant contexts must be built up *in the mind of the* *hearer* (or wired in by evolution: some of us animals are *wired* to wire ourselves that way upon the encounter with certain "experiences" or "linguistic signifieds," such as learning to walk upright or learning to speak) through experiences, for any subsequent interpretation to take place, whether curiosity or fear, recognition, prediction, or negotiation ("I don't want to get wet. Let's go inside. Listen to that . . ." "I *am* listening. Hey, we can make it to Margaret's before it really comes down . . .") is the function.* But mammals in general and primates in particular – as well as whales, dolphins, and Octopoda† – seem to have a knack for learning. Because, until recently, there has been no pressing need to understand the complex mechanics behind some of evolution's effects, that's why many of us don't – though we are capable of learning and, with the help of writing, remembering. There is also an educational, stabilizing superstructure, however, in which intervention can reasonably occur, and where it is possible to stabilize necessary discourses with the help of beneficent

---

*[CopyEd:] *What a rich, evocative sentence this incredibly long, complex – indeed, Johnsonian – one was.*

†[CopyEd:] *As an order this is capped. Or did you mean octopi?*

[SRD:] For years I saw the plural [the various species of octopi] written as Octopodia. But I'm not sure, and you seem to be, so I'll go along with you.

technologies—if you allow cultures to learn in their own way. But this must be both an active and a passive process. This is not cultural relativism (which always moves toward a passive approach that ignores learning and tends toward a dominant destructive approach to behavior, which is sometimes confused *with* learning) but cultural respect—which acknowledges that learning/teaching is always an intervention in the elements that comprise culture, during which both sides must learn if there is to be beneficent change. There is a difference between dialogue-and-respect and imposition-and-domination. And if many more of us don't start to understand those process effects and their imperfections as well as their successes, soon, directly or indirectly, we'll kill each other and ourselves off. It's that simple. The fact that—from mice (who squeak) to mastodons (who trumpeted), bats to beavers, giraffes (who mostly listen but sometimes mew) to gerbils (who chitter), pigeons (who coo) to primates (who grunt, growl, laugh, cry, or talk)—so many creatures share an auditory form of data emission and reception (i.e., hearing and making more or less informative noises; though we all do different things with them) attests to its efficacy for multiple tasks at every level of development as well as to our genetic connectedness over the past 250 million years since the early Triassic and before and the incredibly intricate road to language that a purely synchronic linguistics is inadequate to untangle without a great deal more extension into semiotics, animal and human, and their evolutionary history, much of which is lost.

Given that we have separate brains, that we can "communicate" as much as we can is quite amazing—but don't let your amazement make you forget that "communication" begins as a metaphor for an effect (a door that opens directly from one room to another, a hall that leads from one place in a building to another) but is thus neither a complete nor an accurate description of many things that occur with sound-making and sound-gathering. The fact that so many different creatures have eyes, ears, and kinesthetic reception systems speaks of the efficacy of these effects as well as the genetic relationships among us since before they and their precursors—from gills, extraneous jawbones, and light-sensitive spots on algae and the forerunners of nerves themselves—evolved over millions of generations. That is an index of their usefulness in this landscape. Bear that in mind, and you may start to perceive how complex the process is and why language is *only* the effect that something has passed from person to person, creature to creature, from landscape to creature, whether from speech or in writing or by touch or through any sound—or perceptible signs.

As Gaddis's Basil Valentine remarked, we must treat other people as if they exist, because perhaps they do—though we've gotten a lot more biological and neurological evidence *that* they do. Because of this evidence, the force behind that "perhaps" has strengthened to a strong "probably," though in theory we haven't gotten much further. The similarities and differences from which—neurologically speaking—we learn to interpret the world, unto birth and death, comfort and discomfort, safety and danger, pleasure and pain, and the existence of other people and other creatures and other minds and—whatever ours is—other sexualities and orientations and the worldscapes we share are all still effects, even as they form our only access to the life, the world, the multiverse they create for us. But they would appear to be extremely useful effects for keeping us alive and functioning in our nanosection of a nanosection of that multiverse—that is, if what many of us take to be failures of tolerance among the general deployments and our own employments of these effects of difference don't lead to our destruction.

~

Now that we've had a romp through space, time, and a general ecological agape, which—since Poe obliged an audience of sixty with a talk taken from his then-unpublished *Eureka: A Prose Poem*—we still expect certain sorts of imaginative writers to indulge from time to time, I can tell the following without, I hope, its taking on more critical weight than it can bear: an anecdote that pleases me and makes me smile. For (largely) that's what it is. (The indirect gesturing toward metaphysics is done with for the nonce. And, no, we can't say anything about it directly, which is probably why it takes so long to suggest anything about it at all; and, no, we are still never outside it . . .)

All three books of my *Fall of the Towers* trilogy sold.

Every once in a while, even today, someone writes about them: "Hey, these are interesting—certainly better than I ever thought they would be . . ."

I don't make too much of it.

Still, the trilogy was the favorite of a young man who wrote subtle and involving avant-garde fiction, published by a very respectable press, and also of a sharp young woman who wrote crafted and exciting science fiction—and, in his green T-shirt and his orange rubber glove, of my neighborhood New York sanitation worker.

Before he let go of my shoulder, though, he held me long enough to say that *They Fly at Çiron* — which had just come out in paperback — was his *second* favorite work of mine: a possibility for a similarity, or even for a partial congruence having arisen from his encounter with the text in his mind and from the very different encounter with it in mine, but no certainty, no identity . . .

I smiled. "Why, thank you for taking the time to tell me — about both. That's very nice of you."

Glancing at the glove, he dropped his hand back to his side. "Oh, sure. Anytime, I guess. You're welcome. I'm glad it's okay . . ." He told me about the magazine in which, two weeks before, he'd seen my picture and read its few paragraphs about me. He was a black American man like myself, which meant we'd shared many experiences and much cultural history. He was a black American man like myself, which meant his world and his upbringing were unique, as were mine. For all our human species' similarities, if we look carefully enough, uniqueness — fingerprints, retinal patterns, the synaptic links in our three billion brain cells, genetic variations in both essential and nonessential genetic material which reflect the different specificity each of us inhabits and our ancestors inhabited (i.e., it didn't kill us in that particular landscape before we could pass it on), even if we live in houses next to one another, or in the same house in the same family—is our most widely shared trait. Did that have anything to do with his stopping me? Possibly. In the twenty-five seconds we spoke, the next thing he let me know was how much he liked Octavia Butler's work. "*Kindred* . . . ? Those stories in *Blood Child*?" he asked. "*Patternmaster* . . . ?"

I nodded, smiling.

"Did you ever meet her?"

"She was a student of mine, many years ago," I told him.

"Oh, wow," he declared. "That's amazing! She was?"

"That's right. She was discovered by a white Jewish-born writer, Harlan Ellison, who was running a special program in Los Angeles, and encouraged her to come to the place where I and a number of other SF writers were teaching."

"I didn't know that."

"Well—" I laughed—"now you do."

For a moment he frowned. "Hey, I like his work, too." Then frown relaxed into a smile.

"So do I." I didn't mention how many other SF writers I'd taught over the years—or that Harlan had or any of the other writers and editors who had taught at Clarion, including several times Butler herself, at both Clarion East and Clarion West.

The article had mentioned that I was black— and gay. It hadn't mentioned that my wife and I, though divorced, had raised a daughter. (Or that, for several important years, forty other gay men and their children had helped me.) I was wondering if he had a family when he added, "Great meeting you. Hey, I gotta get back to work."

I called, "Thanks again. So long . . . !" while he loped off past the blue plastic recycling tubs that had already been emptied, to follow the once-white Isuzu refuse collection truck up the street, on which, above and outside the hopper, someone had wired a stuffed, grubby bear.

If you enjoyed *Çiron,* too, I am happy. My apologies, if you didn't. But maybe the extension of this anecdote here will suggest a further explanation for the sanitation worker's reaction, not so different from why Professor Clareson enjoyed *Beta-2.*

Initially, at the conclusion of this note, I'd planned to discuss the alphabet and how what started, after all, as a random collection of signs for sounds developed into such a powerful ordering tool.

Older alphabets, such as Hebrew and Greek, begin, in effect, A, B, G: *aleph, beth, gamil . . . , alpha, beta, gamma . . .*; which suggests a great deal about the history of written language, because so many of those alphabets from that relatively small arc of the world share so many sequences with each other, which means contact between the cultures: the Arabic *abjad* has several orders, two of which begin a, b, d, (*'abjad, hawwaz, ḥuṭṭī*) and two of which begin a, b, t. (We would have neither algebra—which is an Arabic word—nor the use of the Hindu zero, nor the names of so many of our stars without the Arabic language and its cultural flowering through the centuries, in poetry, science, medicine, mathematics, and astronomy.)* Other writing systems, which developed in different places—China and India, Korea and Malaysia, Central and South America—are as rich and as creative as any of the "classic six" (up through much of the nineteenth century, these included Latin, Greek, Hebrew, and Arabic, along with Sanskrit and Aramaic) but work differently, sometimes at very fundamental levels. My first idea was to go on with what an alphabetic ordering could

---

*[CopyEd:] *For that matter, we wouldn't have Aristotle if the Arab writers hadn't translated him.*

accomplish and what it couldn't. As I began drafting my argument, however, I got caught up in still another meditation on "social evolution," an idea I distrust as much as I believe in what we call Darwinian evolution, a distrust for which the huge collapse of the timeframe in "social" evolution is only one bit of the evidence against it—that is to say, which reduces it to a misleading and highly abusable metaphor instead of an efficient explanation of another effect, another illusion, which often contravenes what biological evolution itself so overwhelmingly suggests. But that seemed a bit off-topic for where I wanted this consideration to go.

I decided, therefore, to go back instead to some advice I'd encountered by the time, in Amherst, I settled down to do the work—the rewriting—on *They Fly at Çiron.* (I'd dedicated *Çiron* to my life-partner Dennis, and, after twenty-five years together, I included him in the dedication to an omnibus reprint, as well.) The advice was helpful to me; very helpful. But like all and any writerly advice, it didn't *replace* the work. If I'd only applied it to the textural surface rather than to the fundamental narrative logic, it would have resulted in more confusion (and perhaps it did), whether I was writing fiction or nonfiction. It had to be a guide for where—and the way—to do the work, which, throughout, habit demanded I do as non-habitually as I could. It also suggests why, today, the latest version of *Çiron* is three times as long as the text I salvaged from the old manuscript I'd carried with me from New York to Amherst, and why it has six characters—one of whom is a garbageman—who weren't in the first version at all.

The 1925 Nobel Prize—winning Irish playwright and critic (though he lived much of his life in England) George Bernard Shaw was a great favorite of an astonishing American writer, Joanna Russ, whom I was privileged to have as a friend from the middle sixties until her death in 2011. Though we met only six or seven times, our letters back and forth starting in 1967 fill cartons. She was an enthusiast both of Shaw's plays and of his criticism, musical and dramatic. From adolescence on I'd enjoyed Shaw's theater, but Russ was the first to remind me of his other pieces, some of which I had been lucky enough to have read before on my own, so that I could reread them in the twin illuminations of her knowledge and enthusiasm.

After she started writing, Russ enrolled as a student at the Yale Drama School. Among the things Shaw had said, years before, in a letter to a younger friend that Russ once passed on to me: When actors are told that they are taking too much time to say their lines and that, because the play is too long, they should speed up or even cut the lines, often the better advice is to slow things down even more. Frequently, what makes parts of it seem muddy, slow, or unnecessary is that the development is too compressed for the audience to follow. Expand it and make the articulations of that development sharper and clearer to the listeners. Then the play will give the effect of running *more* quickly and smoothly and what before were "slow" sections will now no longer drag.

That can apply not only to reading texts but to the texts themselves. (Not to mention prefaces, afterwords, and footnotes.) In the imaginary gardens of poetry (with their real toads), Marianne Moore found, famously, that cutting was almost always "the instantaneous solution."

In a world where cutting is seen as so much easier and the audience is far too overvalued—and simultaneously underestimated (the audience is, before all else, ourselves, the readers)—Shaw's suggestion is also important. One of the things that makes it important is how rarely you will hear it or anything like it these days, which is why I've ended with it. It's one way, but only one, to guide the work I must always return to.

A good question with which to begin that kind of revision is: If I set aside, at least momentarily, what I hoped I was writing about when I first put all this down, what is this text in front of me actually about that interests *me?* How can I make that clearer, more comprehensible, and more dramatic to myself? Can I dramatize or clarify it without betraying it?

(And suppose I can't . . . ?)

In revising even this sketchy guide through what is finally a maze of mirrors, several times that's been my question here.

If, like me, you are someone who reads the preface and afterword before you tackle the text between — and often I do, then go on to chuckle over how little they relate to what falls before or after, the world, the text — now, however abruptly, I will stop to let you go on to read as you wish, the world which contains the landscapes you live in as well as the texts you are reading, and of which, for better or for worse, however briefly, all you see and I see are a part. Who knows if there might be or might not be something between these covers that later you'll want to read again? Again, I cannot know.

But I can hope.

We can even think about how my or your hope inspires you, if we will also talk about why it guarantees nothing, neither to the young nor to the old, even though that's one of the things books are presumably for. That's why they have margins, in which (in a sense) prefaces and afterwords (and footnotes) are written. And when you encounter the flaws in the texts here (and you will), you can decide whether or not Shaw's advice applies, or if they require more or less — or simply other — work.

§67: Readers of my Return to Nevèrÿon series may recognize the above as relating to the "Naming, Listing, and Counting Theory" that occasionally crystallizes in one or another of the series' appendices.

George Bernard Shaw's *The Quintessence of Ibsenism* (1891), *The Perfect Wagnerite* (1898), *The Intelligent Woman's Guide to Socialism and Capitalism* (1928) with all its new prefaces and notes and introductions only slight less so, and *The Black Girl in Search of God* (1932) are all still entertaining as well as informative; as is reading his plays and their extraordinary prefaces.

Well, I too, like Horace, write because I believe it is possible — sometimes — for one to educate while one delights.

§68: Sometimes I write because there's a crisis, and I want to talk about it. Sometimes I write because there is no crisis, and I don't want to get out of the habit of writing. Sometimes I write because I have an idea I'd like to try out. At other times, I write because I have no idea at all, and I want to see what will happen if I simply start writing from my thoughts . . .

Philadelphia
*July 4, 2019**

---

*[CopyEd:] *Since this book is being published in 2021, perhaps delete the place and date? And thank you for this eloquent, insightful, delightful glimpse into your extraordinary creative process.*

[SRD:] You're most welcome. But no *way* may you omit the place/date subscription at the end!!! When I finish a book as a reader, I want to know when and where it was written and completed, and I do not want to have to go flipping back to the title page and make my way through a lot of small print with alternate dates for various editions to choose from. Please. That's why the place-date subscription is here: that's where I want to read it. Many and most sincere thanks to you for all of your work, your patience with me, and your suggestions. For the past fifteen years, though, this has been a smaller or large bone of contention with every book I published. I think it is the sign of distrust of the notion that there will *be* a future.

ACKNOWLEDGMENTS

Some of the anecdotes in this piece I have told before in slightly different form in previous works: "A *Paradoxa* Interview: Experimental Writing/Texts & Questions," in *About Writing* (Middletown: Wesleyan University Press, 2006), *The Motion of Light in Water* (Minneapolis: University of Minnesota Press, 2004), and the Afterword of *A, B, C: Three Short Novels* (New York: Vintage, 2015).